Joseph H. Allen, James B. Greenough

A Method of Instruction in Latin

being a companion and guide in the study of Latin grammar

Joseph H. Allen, James B. Greenough

A Method of Instruction in Latin
being a companion and guide in the study of Latin grammar

ISBN/EAN: 9783337870997

Printed in Europe, USA, Canada, Australia, Japan

Cover: Foto ©Paul-Georg Meister /pixelio.de

More available books at **www.hansebooks.com**

A METHOD

OF

INSTRUCTION IN LATIN

BEING

A COMPANION AND GUIDE IN THE STUDY OF LATIN GRAMMAR

WITH ELEMENTARY
INSTRUCTION IN READING AT SIGHT, EXERCISES IN
TRANSLATION AND WRITING, NOTES,
AND VOCABULARY

BY

J. H. ALLEN AND J. B. GREENOUGH

BOSTON
GINN BROTHERS
1875

PREFACE.

THIS book has been prepared under the conviction that too much time is generally spent upon the study of Latin Grammar. It is intended to be learned by a good class under good instruction — where this is made the chief study — in three months, or, if not so much time daily can be afforded, in six; and, if well learned, it will prepare the student for any college entrance-examination in this subject.

A familiar and accurate knowledge of *forms* is first of all necessary, and is here fully provided for, by noting in detail and progressively the essential parts of the etymology to be learned. To learn the grammar *in bulk*, as is still sometimes attempted, we consider one of the most unhappy departures from the true method of a classical education.

Some special features of this book may require to be pointed out.

First, we have desired that all the instruction given should be *founded on a strictly scientific etymology*. With this view, we begin with the fundamental distinction of Root and Stem, — the basis of all true philology, — training the learner's eye from the start to recognize the radical forms of the language. Again, in indicating the quantity of syllables, we have marked all vowels naturally long, made so by laws of inflection ("vowel-increase"), or by certain combinations, as *nf* and *ns*. With the same view, we have called special attention to the development of the verb-stem from the root, and have given unusually full instruction on the principles of derivation and composition of words. The Lessons in this portion are not intended to indicate how much is to be learned at once, but only to divide subjects, and they may of course be subdivided at pleasure.

The etymological part is accompanied with exercises upon each group of forms in detail. To avoid lengthening the exercises in mutilated extracts, the syntax is not so presented. Our view is that the learning of rules of syntax is useless except as explanatory of cases which the learner meets with in actual practice. A selection of passages is therefore given which affords one or more examples of all the syntactical principles considered necessary to start with in reading a Latin author, except two or three. A list of the sections of grammar containing all the necessary principles is given, — something less than a quarter part in bulk of the entire Syntax, — and this list is referred to by figures in each case. It is expected that the teacher will make the occurrence of the example the occasion to teach (or to require the pupil to learn) the general doctrine of the subject, so that after finishing these lessons he may have a body of syntax sufficient to begin authors. The details of syntax are of course to be learned in the course of reading and by exercises in composition, for which a book is now in preparation as a sequel to this.

In the selection of examples we have rigidly avoided the artificial school-text-book Latin, which, with illusive simplicity and ease, only serves to "push forward" the difficulties which will, at any rate, meet the student on the threshold of his real reading. While we have sought to make the exercises easy and progressive, we have given (with very rare exceptions) only sentences from classical authors. The more difficult Selections which follow are, it is hoped, sufficiently annotated to serve the uses of an introductory book. They may, however, be taken at sight, if preferred, with oral exposition from the teacher; and, if well learned, ought to prepare the pupil to take up any ordinary Latin prose without difficulty.

Teachers will find the suggestions on reading at sight new, and it is hoped will constantly practise it with their assistance. They will be surprised at the result. We are persuaded that no thorough classical training, nor the full advantage of such training as we have, can be generally secured in this country until this practice becomes common.

With the aid of the Supplement (taken from the authors' Latin Grammar) this book may be easily used in connection with any other grammar, though, of course, more conveniently with that to which it is especially adapted.

CAMBRIDGE, January 1, 1875.

CONTENTS.

	PAGE
INTRODUCTION: 1. Pronunciation	1
2. Elementary Definitions	3
LESSON 1. The Root and Stem	5
2. Gender and Declension	6
3. First Declension of Nouns	7
4. Second Declension of Nouns	8
5. Adjectives of First and Second Declensions	9
6. Simple Sentence: Subject and Predicate	11
7. " Object Accusative	13
8. " Questions; Conjunctions	14
9. Third Declension of Nouns	16
10. Adjectives of the Third Declension	20
11. Comparison of Adjectives	21
12. Fourth and Fifth Declensions of Nouns	23
13. Pronouns: Personal and Demonstrative	24
14. " Relative, Interrogative, and Indefinite	25
15. Numerals	28
16. Verb-Forms	29
17. The Verb ESSE, *to be*	29
18. Moods and Tenses	30
19. Regular Verb: 1st Conjugation, *Active*	31
20. " " " " *Passive*	32
21. " " " " *Noun and Adjective Forms*	34
22. Regular Verb: 2d Conjugation	36
23. " " 3d Conjugation	38
24. " " 4th Conjugation	39
25. Deponent Verbs	41
26. Irregular, Defective, and Impersonal Verbs	42
27. Formation of Verb-Stems	44
28. Particles	45

	PAGE
CONSTRUCTIONS OF SYNTAX	46
DERIVATION OF WORDS	52
READING AT SIGHT	56
SELECTIONS : 1. *A Haunted House*	63
2. *A Sharper of Syracuse*	64
3. *The Vale of Enna*	65
4. *The Earth is made for Man*	67
5. *The Heavens declare a Creator*	69
6. *An Active Old Age*	69
INDEX OF CONSTRUCTIONS	71
NOTES	71
VOCABULARY : 1. English and Latin	75
2. Latin and English	83

SUPPLEMENT (from Grammar): Outline of Syntax.
                          Synopsis of Constructions.

INTRODUCTION.

1. — PRONUNCIATION.

THERE is at present a strong tendency, among the best scholars, to pronounce Latin (as well as Greek) *phonetically*, giving to each letter of the alphabet the one sound which by the best authority most nearly represents that given it by Romans of the classic ages. These sounds are given in the grammar (§ 2, 1). Observing the rules of accent, it is only necessary to give each letter its proper enunciation. This is by far the easiest and simplest way. It may be acquired by any intelligent person, with a good ear, in ten minutes; though practice will be required to make the reading fluent and agreeable.

Many persons, however, prefer to retain the English Method, so called; that is, the practice which has prevailed, with some variation, in England and among ourselves, for the last two or three centuries. In general, the following direction is sufficient. *Read a Latin sentence just as if the words were English, observing the rules of accent* (§ 4), *and bearing in mind that there are no silent letters*. This single precept would probably give a pronunciation as correct and about as uniform as can be had from any number of arbitrary rules. A few special points necessary to be observed are given in the grammar (§ 2, 2). To read Latin easily and well is an accomplishment which must be taught orally, and acquired by practice. The directions which follow, accordingly, are *not intended to be studied by the pupil*, but to serve as a guide in cases of doubt.

1. The chief difference between Latin (pronounced as in English) and English is that the former has no silent letters. *Every vowel makes a syllable;* except in the combinations **ae, oe, au, eu, ei, ui,** and **u** before a vowel, and these are separate when marked with the diæresis. Thus *di-es, ma-re, pau-pe-ri-ē-i.*

2. The vowels always have their English sounds: —

a as in *mane* or *man.*	**ae** } as **e**.
e „ *be* or *bed.*	**oe** }
i „ *find* or *fin.*	**au** as *aw* in *awe.*
o „ *note* or *not.*	**eu** as *ew* in *hew.*
u „ *tune* or *tun.*	**ei** } as **i**.
y as **i**.	**ui** }

3. An unaccented **i** before another vowel is in almost all cases changed into its semivowel **y**. In the same cases as in English this **y** blends with the preceding consonant, making the sound of *sh*, as in *Maia* (Ma-ya), *Pompēius* (Pom-pé-yus), *Harpyia* (Harpí-ya), *socius* (so-shus), *vitium* (vish-yum), *Asia* (A-shya).

Except such words as *Fabius* (Fá-be-us), where the **y** is less distinct; so *Sextius, flectier,* where it is hardly distinguishable at all. Practice must be the guide in these cases.

4. Of the two sounds of the vowels above given the long sound (so called) ends a syllable, the short (" stopped ") sound is followed by a consonant: as *pa-ter* (pay-ter), *mag-nus* (mag-nus), *de-dit* (de-dit), *reg-num* (reg-num). But **a** at the end of an unaccented syllable has an obscure sound like English **er** in *dancer: stella* (stellar).

5. The combinations **quad** and **quart** are pronounced as in English (*quart*); **arr** is pronounced as in *Harry;* **es** at the end of plural words has the long sound: *pes* (pease), *pares* (pay-reze), *nos* (noce); **post** (with its compounds) is pronounced like the same word in English.

6. The consonants are pronounced as in English. Thus, **c** is soft (*s*) before **e, i, y, ae, oe, eu**. Elsewhere it is hard (*k*), and it blends with **u** in nearly the same cases as in English, as *socius, conscius* (pronounced *shus*); **ch** is always *k*, as in *charta, máchina;* **g** is soft (*j*) and hard in the same situations respectively as **c**.

7. **S** is usually hard (sharp as in *saw*). It is sonant (soft, *z*) at the end of a word, after **e, ae, au, n, r,** as *pes, audes, mons, pars, trans* (even in composition). A few other words have also sonant **s** (*z*), as *causa, rosa.*

8. **X** has the sound of *z* at the beginning and of *ks* at the end of syllables: as, *Xerx-es, pax.*

Since many of the sounds depend upon the open or close syllables, the following rules for the division of syllables may be observed, which are, however, the regular rules in English.

9. A vowel *not accented* and a penultimate vowel in any case *complete their syllables without* a following single consonant or mute with *l* or *r*, as *socius, ratio*. (This rule applies when the number of syllables is reduced by rule 3 above.)

10. A vowel *accented*, not penultimate, requires the following single consonant, or divides the combination of mute with *l* or *r*.

11. But a following i and e attract a consonant rather than an accented ā, ō, ŏ, preceding; as *me-di-á-tor, haé-re-o pá-tri-us.*— u, on the other hand, repels a following consonant, as *lú-ci-dus, dú-ri-us*.

12. A single consonant after any accented vowel except the penultimate is joined with that vowel. A mute and liquid in this position are separated. In other cases a single consonant or a mute and liquid belong to the following vowel.

13. Two consonants (except a mute and *l* or *r* as above) are divided: as, *mag-nus, cor-pus*.

14. Of three or more consonants, the last (or a mute with *l* or *r* as above) is given to the following syllable.

15. A compound word is divided between the parts if the first ends in a consonant, otherwise it follows the rules for single words: as, *prod-est, circum-esse, prae-sto, ego-met, pro-sum*.

2. — ELEMENTARY DEFINITIONS.

1. GRAMMAR treats of the different forms of words (ETYMOLOGY), and the mode of connecting them in speech (SYNTAX).

2. Words are either Nouns, Adjectives, Pronouns, Verbs, Participles, Adverbs, Prepositions, Conjunctions, or Interjections. These are called PARTS OF SPEECH.

3. Words like *Cæsar, consul, temple, virtue,* which are names of persons, things, or ideas, are called NOUNS.

4. Words like *brave, loud, strong,* which express qualities, are called ADJECTIVES.

5. Words which indicate any person or thing, without either naming or describing, are called PRONOUNS. These include PERSONAL, as *I, thou, we, he, they;* and ADJECTIVE, as *these, those* (Demonstrative), *my, your* (Possessive), *who, which* (Relative or Interrogative).

6. Words like *build, fight, stand, be, suffer,* which express actions or conditions, are called VERBS.

7. Words like *conquering, going, gone, beaten,* which describe by means of actions or conditions, are called PARTICIPLES.

8. Words like *nobly, well, very, here, now, to-day,* which define an action or quality in manner, place, time, or the like, are called ADVERBS.

9. Words like *for, with, by, against,* which show the relation between a noun and other words in the sentence, are called PREPOSITIONS.

10. Words like *and, or, if, but, then,* which connect words or sentences together, are called CONJUNCTIONS.

11. Some words as *where, while, till, nevertheless,* both define as adverbs and connect as conjunctions. These are called ADVERBIAL CONJUNCTIONS.

12. Words like *ah! ho! alas!* are mere exclamations, and are not strictly parts of speech, but are called INTERJECTIONS.

METHOD.

Lesson I.

The Root and Stem.

READ carefully § 5, 1 and 2, of the Grammar.*

1. Distinguish the *Root* and the *Stem*, together with their meanings (as in § 5), of the following:—

vōx, *a voice;* vōcis, *of a voice.*
vŏcāmus, *we call;* vŏcātis, *you call;* vŏcāvī, *I have called.*
vŏcātiōnis, *of a calling;* vŏcātiōnī, *to a calling.*
vōcālis, *belonging to a voice;* vōcŭla, *a feeble voice.*

2. Determine, by comparison with each other and with the preceding, the *root* of the following:—

ămor, *love;* ămāmus, *we love;* ămātor, *lover;* ămāvī, *I have loved;* ămat, *he loves;* ămānt, *they love.*

Let the teacher point out the *stems* of these words, and the meaning of the *terminations*.

3. Determine the *root* and *stem* of the following words:—

fert, *he bears;* est, *he is* (§ 5, 2. *c*).
rĕgit, *he rules* (§ 5, 2. *c³*); rectus, *straight (ruled);* rēx, *king* (§ 1, 3. *f³*); rēgis, *of a king;* rēgŭla, *a rule;* regnum, *royal power;* dīrigit, *he directs;* arrectus, *roused.*
dux, *leader;* dūcit, *he leads;* dūxērunt, *they led;* dŭci, *to a leader;* redŭces (plur.), *brought back.*
frăgĭlis, *frail;* frangit, *he breaks;* fractus, *broken;* fractūra, *breakage;* frăgor, *crash;* frēgit, *he broke.*
cădit, *he falls;* cĕcĭdit, *he fell;* cāsus, *chance;* accĭdit, *it happens.*

For the change of vowels in the foregoing, see § 1, 3. *a, b.*

For the change of consonants, compare § 1, 3. *f.*

N. B. In the examples hereafter given, only the *long vowels* will, in general, be marked. Those not marked, whether or not long by position (§ 3, 2. *d*), are to be considered short by nature.

* The references are to the Sections of Allen and Greenough's Latin Grammar.

Lesson 2.

Gender and Declension.

1. LEARN § 6, 1, with *a* and *c*; 2, with *c*; 3; § 7, and § 8, 1, with *a*; 2. *a*, *b*, *c*.

Questions on the above.

1. What is Natural Gender? 2. What is Grammatical Gender? 3. What names are masculine? 4. What feminine? 5. What forms of expression are neuter? 6. What is Common Gender? 7. Repeat the names of Cases in their usual order. 8. Define the use of each. 9. How many Declensions of nouns are there? 10. How distinguished? 11. Give the genitive ending of each. 12. What is the rule for finding the Stem?

2. Notice that Latin has six cases with a relic of a seventh, where English has only three. Consequently, many relations are expressed by case alone, which in English require to be translated by means of prepositions. In translating from Latin into English, the following observations will be found useful: —

a. The Genitive may usually be translated by the Possessive, or by the preposition OF, and is usually connected with a Noun or Adjective: as, **timor belli**, *fear of war;* **avidus laudis**, *greedy of glory.*

b. The Dative is usually connected with a Verb or Adjective, and may be translated TO or FOR. It often, however, corresponds to the English Objective: as, **cārus amīcīs**, *dear to friends;* **nocet inimīcīs**, *he harms his enemies.*

c. The Accusative is regularly connected with a Verb or Preposition, and is translated most commonly by the Objective.

d. The Vocative is translated by the simple Nominative.

e. The Ablative is used with Verbs and Prepositions, and may oftenest be translated BY, WITH (means or instrument), AT (time and place), FROM, OF (cause and separation); with prepositions, by the Objective: as, **occīsus ferrō**, *slain with the sword;* **dīs satus**, *sprung from the gods;* **tertiā hōrā**, *at the third hour.*

f. The Locative is translated ON, AT, IN (time or place): as, **humī**, *on the ground;* **vesperī**, *at evening.*

The meanings of the cases are so various that the context must very often determine the particular one. (See § 50, 3. N.)

Lesson 3.

First Declension of Nouns.

1. LEARN § 9, with 1, and 2. *c, e.*

Decline **stella**, giving the name and meaning of all the Cases. In like manner decline the following: —

porta (F.), *gate.*
pila (F.), *ball.*
silva (F.), *forest.*
nauta (M.), *sailor.*
dea (F.), *goddess* (2. *e*).
filia (F.), *daughter.*

cōpiae (F. plur.), *forces.*
patria (F.), *native land.*
Rōma (F.), *Rome.*
terra (F.), *earth.*
Athēnae (F. pl.), *Athens.*
via (F.), *way.*

What is the stem of **culpam** (*fault*)? of **rosis** (*rose*)? of **hastæ** (*spear*)? In what case is each?

What is the ablative singular of **hasta**, and how does it differ from the nominative? what is the genitive plural? dative plural? accusative singular? What is the ablative plural of **filia**?

What is the locative form of **Rōma**? of **Athēnæ**? What do these forms mean?

Learn 3, and decline **comētēs, daphnē, Aenēas.**

2. Describe the following forms; that is, give their gender, number, and possible cases, with the meanings: —

1. portam; 2. portā; 3. pilis; 4. cōpiās; 5. Rōmae; 6. filiābus; 7. Athēnis; 8. nautās; 9. deārum; 10. Rōmā; 11. hastārum; 12. cōpiis; 13. daphnēs; 14. comētēn; 15. silvā.

NOTE. — Most forms of nouns or adjectives which the pupil meets in practice are *oblique cases*, of which he must find the nominative and the declension. Since both of these are determined by the stem, it is the simplest way to find the stem first, and then find the nominative (which is in fact a derived form) from that. As the nominative in most nouns of the first declension is the same as the stem, it is not important in that declension; but the advantage of the principle will be seen hereafter.

In the study of inflections, it is well that the learner should accustom himself to *write out the forms in full;* and that this should be made, with the aid of the blackboard, a constant practice in the class-room.

Lesson 4.

Second Declension of Nouns.

1. LEARN § 10, with 1 and 2.

Decline the following, giving the names and meanings of the cases: puer, liber, servus, dōnum.

Notice that these are all declined alike, except in the nom. and voc. singular, and the nom. acc. and voc. plural; and that in the neuter plural all these cases end in ă, as *in all neuter nouns in Latin.*

What is the stem of each?

Form the nominative from the following stems:—

taurŏ- (M.), *bull;* generŏ- (M.), *son-in-law;* aprŏ- (M.), *boar;* humerŏ- (M.), *shoulder;* regnŏ- (N.), *kingdom.*

2. Learn subsection 3. *a, b* (including the lists), and 4. *a, b, c, f.*

Decline (first giving the stem) the following:—

    ager (M.), *field* (6).   fīlius (M.), *son* (4. *b*).
    bellum (N.), *war.*   deus (M.), *a god* (4. *f*).
    oppidum (N.), *town.*   magister (M.), *master.*
    humus (F.), *ground.*   perīculum (N.), *danger.*
    equus (M.), *horse.*   Corinthus (F.), *Corinth.*
    vir (M.), *man* (5. *a*).   Gabii (M. plur.), *Gabii.*

What is the stem of **capris**? in what case or cases can it be? of **generis**? what is the nom. singular? accusative? nom. plural? dative? genitive, of each of these nouns?

What is the stem of **regnum**? What is the genitive singular? plural? the dative plural?

What is the locative form and its meaning of **Corinthus**? of **Tarentum**? of **Gabii**? of **bellum**? of **humus**? of **vesper**?

What is the vocative of **Marcus**? of **Tullius**? of **puer**?

Decline (7. *d*) lotŏs, organŏn, Ulixes.

3. Describe (as before) the following:—

1. virī; 2. taurōrum; 3. deī; 4. equō; 5. caprum; 6. deī (dī); 7. bellōrum; 8. humī; 9. ventō; 10. dīs; 11. virīs; 12. deōs, 13. Tarentī; 14. Gabiīs; 15. fīliīs; 16. magistrōrum; 17. bella; 18. fīlī; 19. vesperī (5, *a*); 20. perīculīs.

Lesson 5.

Adjectives of the First and Second Declensions.

1. LEARN § **16**, with **1** (the teacher explaining the Note), and *a*.

Decline (each gender by itself) the following, first giving the masculine and feminine stems of each: **cārus, miser, āter.**

Observe that the declension of Adjectives of this form is precisely the same with that of the corresponding nouns, **servus, puer, liber; stella, dōnum.**

Decline the above *by cases* (all genders at once).

Decline (in either or both methods) the following, giving first their masculine stem: —

bonus, *good.*	sacer, *sacred.*	meus, *my* (voc. **mī**).
magnus, *great.*	longus, *long.*	nōster, *our.*
parvus, *small.*	grātus, *pleasing.*	multī (plur.), *many.*
līber, *free.*	validus, *strong.*	paucī (plur.), *few.*

2. Learn § **47**, and read Remark.

Decline together the following, making the Adjective agree with the Noun in *gender, number,* and *case:* —

    vir bonus;   hasta valida;
    taurus niger;   bellum longum.

Observe that in Latin a descriptive Adjective generally *comes after the noun*, not before it as in English.

3. Learn the list, with significations, in 1, *b*; and decline the examples.

Observe that these, except **alius**, differ from the regular declension only in the genitive and dative singular. The peculiar forms belong properly to Pronouns, with which these words are allied also in meaning. Learn also the declension of **duo** (page 42), and decline together the following: —

ūnus vir;	ulla porta;	sōlus fīlius;
altera fīlia;	duae hastae;	aliud bellum;
uter equus?	alia via;	ager utervis.

Notice that **utervis** is compounded of **uter** and **vis**, *which* [of the two] *you will;* and that the first part only is declined.

4. Many adjectives in the singular, and most adjectives in the plural, may be used as Nouns, the masculine meaning *men*, the feminine *women*, and the neuter *things* (§ 47, 3, 4): thus,

līber, *a free man.* bonī, *the good.*
amīcus, *a friend.* Latīnī, *the Latins.*
Rōmānus, *a Roman.* Sabīnae, *the Sabine women.*

5. Learn § 46, with the examples; and translate the following phrases: —

Homērus poēta; Rōma patria nostra; Gabiī oppidum.

Notice that the added noun (*in apposition*) does not express any relation such as is mentioned in Lesson 3, but is only another way of describing the same thing.

6. Describe (as before) the following: —

1. fīliō cārō; 2. dōnīs sacrīs; 3. stellās lūcidās; 4. ūnīus librī; 5. nullīs fīliābus; 6. alterī virō; 7. aliūs portae; 8. sacrīs deābus; 9. mī cāre fīlī; 10. aliud regnum; 11. taurīs validīs; 12. urbānum vulgus; 13. tōtum pelagus; 14. duōbus virīs.

Learn the meaning of the following particles: —

et, *and;* sed, *but;* nōn, *not;* etiam, *even.*

Translate into English.

1. Terrae (*Less.* 3, 2. *a*) filius. 2. Pericula belli. 3. Porta oppidi Tarenti. 4. Marci pueri magister. 5. Marce Tulli. 6. Somnia fabularum. 7. Gaius Marius inimicus bonorum. 8. Sthenelus non auriga piger. 9. Mora magnum irae[1] remedium.

[1] The genitive is here to be translated *for* (see last paragraph of Lesson 2).

Write in Latin.

1. Alexander the Great, son of Philip. 2. Italy, the native land of the Latins. 3. Gifts of the good, pleasing to (*Less.* 2, 2. *b*) the gods. 4. Romans (*acc.*), sons of free men. 5. Dear to one, pleasing to many. 6. A great abundance of gold and silver.

Lesson 6.

Simple Sentence: 1. Subject and Predicate.

LEARN § 45, 1 and 2.

1. Every real sentence must contain at least a Subject and a Verb. The Subject of a verb is regularly in the Nominative case (§ 49, 2): as,

> equus currit, *the horse runs.*
> rēgīna sedet, *the queen sits.*

NOTE. — In certain constructions, a verb is put in the infinitive mood, in which case its subject becomes the Accusative (§ 52, 4, *b*).

2. In Latin, the subject may be a personal pronoun contained in the termination of the verb itself: as,

aro, *I plough (am ploughing);* sedēmus, *we sit;* currītis, *you run.*

NOTE. — This is true, in general, only when the verb is of the first or second person. With the third person, a definite subject must be expressed, unless implied in what goes before or follows.

3. Learn the following forms of the verb esse, *to be:* —

PRESENT.

sum, *I am.*	sumus, *we are.*
es, *thou art (you are).*	estis, *you are.*
est, *he (she, it) is.*	sunt, *they are.*

IMPERFECT.

eram, *I was.*	erāmus, *we were.*
erās, *thou wast.*	erātis, *you were.*
erat, *he (she, it) was.*	erant, *they were.*

Upon comparing these examples, the learner will notice that the terminations are alike for each person: thus,

SINGULAR		PLURAL	
1.	-m	1.	-mus
2.	-s	2.	-tis
3.	-t	3.	-nt

These terminations were originally personal pronouns, and still retain their force as such. They run, with some slight changes, through all verbal forms which have persons.

Notice that the plural of courtesy, used in addressing a single person, is not found in Latin. Hence *you are* corresponds both with **es** when one person is addressed, and with **estis** when more than one.

NOTE. — The verb **esse** belongs to no regular conjugation, but its inflection is older than that of the regular verbs; just as in English *love, loved* is the regular, but *know, knew* the older form.

4. The verb **esse** has two meanings, which require different constructions (see § **45**, 2. *b*). When it means *to exist*, it may make a sentence either alone, or with only a subject-nominative: as,

>**est lūna,** *there is a moon.*

But it is also used, like the English *to be*, as a mere *copula* (link) between a subject and a predicate, which are then in the same case (§ **46**, 1. 2): as,

>**magister es,** *you are master.*
>**lūna est lūcida,** *the moon is bright.*

NOTE. — The predicate and copula may, however, both be contained in a Latin verb: as,

>**agricola arat,** *the farmer is ploughing.*
>**portae patēnt,** *the gates are open.*

Translate into English.

1. Pueri sumus. 2. Stellae lucidae erant. 3. Laeti non eramus. 4. Viri boni sunt.[1] 5. Patria nostra non est Roma. 6. Servus perpetuus mercenarius est. 7. Mnesarchus et Dardanus magistri erant (§ **49**, 1) Athenis. 8. Saepe est etiam sub palliolo sordido sapientia. 9. Nullum magnum ingenium sine mixtura dementiae est. 10. Magnorum saevitia bellum est.

---

[1] This sentence may be translated *they* (some persons previously referred to, and implied in the termination) *are good men;* or, *the men are good;* also (considering **sunt** as a substantive verb), *there are good men.* In the first case, **boni** and **viri** are both predicate; in the second, **viri** is subject and **boni** predicate; in the third, both are in the subject.

Write in Latin.

1. Æneas was a good son. 2. We are free [men], not slaves. 3. The early Romans were farmers. 4. Rome was the native city (*fatherland*) of Marcus Tullius. 5. Delay is a cure for anger.

N. B. In writing a Latin sentence, *usually put the verb at the end*. Words in brackets are not to be translated.

Lesson 7.

Simple Sentence: 2. Object-Accusative.

LEARN § 52, and 1.

1. The action of many verbs (called Transitive verbs) passes over upon an object, which must be expressed to complete the sense. This object is in Latin put in the Accusative: as,

vocat filium, *he calls* (his) *son;* **vidēmus stellās,** *we see the stars.*

NOTE.— *a.* With certain verbs, the genitive, dative, or ablative may be used as an object-case, where the corresponding English verbs require the objective.

b. Many verbs transitive in Latin are translated in English by a verb requiring a preposition (intransitive): as, **pecūniam postulo,** *I ask for (demand) money;* **petit aprum,** *he aims at the boar.*

2. Learn the following verb-forms of the First and Second conjugations: —

I.

voco, *I call.*	**vocāmus,** *we call.*
vocās, *you call (thou callest).*	**vocātis,** *you call.*
vocat, *he (she, it) calls.*	**vocānt,** *they call.*

II.

video, *I see.*	**vidēmus,** *we see.*
vidēs, *you see* (thou seest).	**vidētis,** *you see.*
videt, *he (she, it) sees.*	**vident,** *they see.*

Upon comparing these forms, the learner will notice that the first has ā and the second ē before the terminations. These vowels belong to the stem of the verb (see Lesson 1), and are characteristic of two different conjugations called the *first* and *second*. In the first person singular, **voca-o** has been contracted into **voco**.

Like **voco** inflect the following: —

 amo, *love*. **do**, *give*. **laudo**, *praise*.
 aro, *plough*. **juvo**, *help*. **pugno**, *fight*.

Like **video** inflect the following: —

 doceo, *teach*. **noceo**, *injure*. **timeo**, *fear*.
 habeo, *have*. **sedeo**, *sit*. **valeo**, *be strong*.

Translate into English.

1. Ludi magister pueros vocat. 2. Avaritia pecuniae studium habet. 3. Manlius, vir bello egregius, Romanos ad arma vocat. 4. Unus e decemviris, Appius Claudius, puellam plebeiam raptat. 5. Arma habemus non adversus pueros sed adversus armatos. 6. Contra naturam non pugno. 7. Nocet aliquando medicina magis quam juvat. 8. Laudamus claros viros, improbos vituperamus. 9. Lælia, Gai filia, paternam elegantiam habet. 10. Alienis incommodis pauci dolent.

Write in Latin.

1. The boys are fighting. 2. We love (our) children and friends. 3. The sound of the log frightens the silly frogs. 4. The timorous doe fears not the maiden. 5. The ancient comedy teaches wisdom.

Lesson 8.

Simple Sentence: 3. Special Forms.

1. *Questions.*—Learn § **45**, 1, with *a, b, c, d*; and compare § **71**.

a. A Question *of simple fact*, requiring the answer *yes* or *no*, is formed in Latin by adding the syllable **-ne** (*enclitic*) to the emphatic word: as,

 eratne Caesaris amicus? *was he* (in fact) *Cæsar's friend.*
 tūne erās Caesaris amīcus? *were* YOU *a friend of Cæsar?*

NOTE.—Sometimes the interrogative particle is omitted, when no sign of a question appears except in the punctuation (§ **71**, 1, R).

b. A Question asking *of some circumstance about the fact* is formed by prefixing to the sentence an interrogative word. Such words are

quis? *who?* ubi? *where?* quando? *when?* quārē? *why?* quōmodō? *how?* quālis? *of what sort?* quantus? *how great?*

NOTE. — A Question of the latter form becomes an exclamation by omitting the mark of interrogation, or (in speech) by changing the inflection of the voice.

c. When the syllable -ne is added to a negative word, — as **nonne**, — an affirmative answer is expected.

[For other interrogative forms, see § 71, 1, 2.]

2. *Conjunctions.* — ***a.*** Two simple independent sentences are often connected by Conjunctions, and make coördinate clauses (§ 45, 5. *c*) in the same sentence. Such conjunctions are —

et, *and;* **sed**, *but;* **at**, *but yet;* **aut**, **vel**, *or;* **nec** (**neque**), *nor = and not;* **atque** (sometimes **ac** before a consonant), *and besides;* **-que** (*enclitic*) *and.*

b. Of these the following are often repeated in the different parts of the sentence, for the sake of distinction or emphasis : —

et or **-que**, *both . . . and;* **aut** (**vel**), *either . . . or;* **nec** or **neque**, *neither . . . nor.* [See § 43, 2. *a*.]

c. It is very common, in sentences thus made up of two or more members, to express in one part what must be understood in the rest (*ellipsis*) : as,

C. Gracchus amicus plēbis erat, Scīpiōnēs inimīcī [plēbis erant], *Caius Gracchus was a friend of the commons, the Scipios* [were their] *enemies.*

Translate into English.

1. Nonne laudant posteri viros claros? 2. Quanta sunt amicitiae vincula! 3. Videsne novum populum unius viri consilio ortum? 4. Nec optat vir bonus crastinum nec timet. 5. Virtus, Gai Fanni et Quinte

Muci, et conciliat amicitias et confirmat. 6. Miser ergo est Archelaus? 7. Non oculis sed animo videmus. 8. Graeci praeceptis valent, Romani exemplis. 9. Extra invidiam sed non extra gloriam erat. 10. Nihil perpetuum, pauca diuturna sunt.

Write in Latin.

1. Neither Marius nor Sulla was a true friend of the Roman people. 2. Is not virtue a bond of friendship? 3. Do we fear the perils of war? 4. Who praises the bad? Who does not love the good?

Lesson 9.

Third Declension of Nouns.

1. LEARN § 11, i. with 1, 2; ii. iii. with 1, 2, 3.

The Third Declension includes all nouns having stems ending in a consonant ("consonant-stems"), and all those whose stem ends in i ("i- stems"). The consonant-stems are simplest, as the case-endings are added to the stem, and never confounded with it: hence they have one more syllable in the genitive, &c., than in the nominative. [Except pater, māter, frāter, accipiter, which are syncopated: patris for patĕris, etc.]

2. Decline the following Mute-stems (iii.):—

ops, ŏpis (F.), *help.*
princeps, ĭpis (M.), *chief.*
custōs, ōdis (M.), *guard.*
lapis, ĭdis (M.), *stone.*
mīles, ĭtis (M.), *soldier.*
seges, ĕtis (F.), *crop.*

rēx, rēgis (M.), *king.*
rādīx, īcis (F.), *root.*
apex, ĭcis (M.), *peak.*
caput, ĭtis (N.), *head.*
cor, cordis (N.), *heart.*
poēma, ătis (N.), *poem.*

Find the stem and nominative of the following:—

1. opēs; 2. forcipis; 3. pede; 4. lēgibus; 5. pācem; 6. militum; 7. incūdis; 8. corda; 9. poēma (acc.); 10. praesidem; 11. dŭcēs; 12. vădis; 13. quiēte; 14. parietum; 15. virtūtibus; 16. mercēdis; 17. capite, 18. apices; 19. lapide; 20. segete; 21. hiemis; 22. palūdibus; 23. equitēs; 24. laudī.

Third Declension of Nouns.

3. Decline the following Liquid-stems (ii.) : —

consul, ŭlis (M.), *consul.*
nōmen, ĭnis (N.), *name.*
leō, ōnis (M.), *lion.*
virgo, ĭnis (F.), *maiden.*
legiō, ōnis (F.), *legion.*

sanguis, ĭnis (M.), *blood.*
caro, carnis (F.), *flesh* (iii. 4).
senex, senis (M.), *old man.*
mel, mellis (N.), *honey* (ii. *e*).
homo, ĭnis (M.), *man.*

Find the stem and nominative of the following : —

1. hominum; 2. ordines; 3. virginibus; 4. sēmina; 5. delphīnī; 6. Platōnis; 7. cornicines; 8. sanguinem; 9. senibus.

Notice that **sanguis** and **senex** have two stems.

4. Decline the following original **r**- stems : —

pater, tris (M.), *father.*
mulier, ĕris (F.), *woman.*
anser, ĕris (M.), *goose.*
crātēr, ēris (M.), *bowl.*

nectar, ăris (N.), *nectar.*
fulgur, ŭris (N.), *thunderbolt.*
rhētor, ŏris (M.), *rhetorician.*
āēr, āĕris (M.), *air.*

NOTE. — Nouns with these terminations have an original **r**. In almost all other **r**- stems, the **r** takes the place of an original **s**, which is retained in the nominative and the other cases which are like it. In **crātēr** and **āēr**, observe the Greek forms of the accusative singular (**a**), and the nominative and accusative plural (**ĕs, ăs**).

5. Decline the following, in which the stem has been changed from **s**: —

flōs, flōris (M.), *flower.*
honor (honōs), ōris (M.), *honor.*
pulvis, ĕris (M.), *dust.*
tellūs, ūris (F.), *earth.*
iter, itĭnĕris (N.), *journey.*

jecur, jecinŏris (N.), *liver.*
aes, aeris (N.), *copper.*
ebur, ŏris (N.), *ivory.*
corpus, ŏris (N.), *body.*
genus, ĕris (N.), *race.*

NOTE. — All the above classes are *regular consonant stems,* without any trace of **i** in their inflection. Some consonant-stems originally **i**- stems, and having **i** in their inflection, will be given after the real **i**- stems.

6. Decline the following **i**- stems : —

turris (F.), *tower.*
sitis (F.), *thirst* (3, *a*).
secūris (F.), *axe.*
ovis (F.), *sheep.*
clādēs (F.), *disaster.*

mare (N.), *sea.*
rēte (N.), *net.*
calcar (N.), *spur.*
pulvīnar (N.), *cushion.*
vectīgal (N.), *revenue.*

Observe that this class includes all nouns of the third declension which have the same number of syllables in the nominative and genitive (except pater, etc.); also neuters in al and ar, which have lost a final e. They show the i of the stem in the following forms: —

1. All have the genitive plural in -ium;
2. All neuters have the nom. and acc. plural in -ia;
3. The accusative plural (M. or F.) is often written -īs;
4. The accusative singular (M. or F.) sometimes ends in -im;
5. The ablative singular of all neuters, and of many masculines and feminines, ends in -ī (see lists *a* and *b*, p. 18 of Grammar).

7. Describe the following forms (as in Lesson 3), giving first the stem and nominative.

1. tussim; 2. febrim; 3. rāvī (abl.); 4. ignī; 5. clādem; 6. imbrium; 7. puppis; 8. sēdium; 9. animālia; 10. navālibus; 11. tribūnālī; 12. exemplārium; 13. Tiberim; 14. amussim; 15. lintrī; 16. imbrēs; 17. marī; 18. rētibus.

Decline together the following: —

1. bonus cīvis; 2. turris alta; 3. amnis lātus; 4. rēte rārum; 5. clādēs magna; 6. ovēs multae; 7. restis longa; 8. animal nigrum; 9. secūris acūta; 10. novus homo; 11. magnum opus; 12. mulier Sabīna; 13. Rōmāna virgō; 14. senex doctus; 15. mīles validus; 16. Marcus Tullius Cicero consul.

8. Some nouns originally i- stems retain traces of the i declension. Learn iii. note, with 2, *c*, 3, *c*; and decline the following: —

arx, arcis (F.), *citadel*.	lis, lītis (M.), *lawsuit*.
aetās, ātis (F.), *age*.	mūs, mūris (M.), *mouse*.
faucēs, ium (F.), *throat*.	os, ossis (N.), *bone*.
gens, gentis (F.), *nation*.	urbs, urbis (F.), *city*.

NOTE. — The genitive plural in many of this class is uncertain, and the ablative in ī is very rare; so that, except those mentioned (including monosyllables with *stems ending in two consonants*), it is better to follow the consonant declension.

Decline bōs, nix, vīs, Juppiter (iii. 4).

N. B. The teacher may (if he think desirable) require the Rules for Gender on pp. 23, 24; but it seems best to learn each word or class of words by itself, through practice in reading and composition.

Translate into English.

1. Militem vana gloriae imago tenet. 2. Nemo vere aestimat tempus. 3. Habet philosophus amplas opes. 4. Caesar jus crudelitatemque victoriae temperat. 5. Rex honores dignis dat. 6. Non est voluptas sine virtute. 7. Medicina etiam sceleratis opem ministrat. 8. Apud Epicureos virtus voluptatum ministra est. 9. Genus ex alto sanguine deorum habemus. 10. Agricolam annonae caritas delectat. 11. Di operum humanorum sunt testes. 12. Mira fulminis opera sunt: fulmina fatorum ordinem nuntiant; olei et unguenti teter post fulmen odor est. 13. Fata nullae preces commovent. 14. Eloquentiae pretium auget litium numerus. 15. Institores delicatarum mercium juventus corrupta locupletat. 16. Non hospes ab hospite tutus erat, non socer a genero; fratrum quoque gratia rara erat. 17. Boves et equos, ibes, accipitres, aspidas, crocodilos, piscīs, canes, lupos, feles, multas praeterea beluas, barbari in deorum numero habent.

Write in Latin.

1. An omen recalls the superstitious man from a journey. 2. Young men delight in the precepts (*abl.*) of the old. 3. Is there any animal without a heart? 4. I approve seriousness in old age, [*but*] bitterness by no means. 5. How great opportunities has friendship! 6. Not the guards of the citadel, doubtless valiant soldiers; not the dogs, a creature uneasy at nightly sounds; but the sacred geese of Juno wake, scream [*and*] save the city.

Lesson 10.

Adjectives of the Third Declension.

1. Learn § 16, 2 (with the list in *a*) and 3, with *a;* and decline the accompanying examples.

Notice: 1. That these are inflected as i-stems throughout, except that the accusative singular is never found in **im**, while those in 2. *a*, differ from other i-stems only in having the nominative and vocative singular of the masculine in **er**. All other adjectives in **er** belong to 3. *c* (consonant declension).

2. That the adjectives in 3, *a*, have i inflections in the same cases as the preceding, except that the ablative has e as well as i. [Notice rare exceptions in 3. *c*.] In other respects, these adjectives are declined precisely like the corresponding nouns (consonant-stems) of the third declension.

2. Learn 3. *b*, and decline the examples.

Notice that these comparatives have no forms of the i declension, except i along with e in the ablative singular. [But plus, with its compound **complūrēs**, is an exception.]

Decline the following: —

  omnis, *every;* plur. *all.*   **dīves**, *rich.*
  brevis, *short.*   **potēns**, *powerful.*
  facilis, *easy.*   **praeceps**, *headlong.*
  fortis, *brave.*   **pauper**, *poor.*
  gravis, *heavy.*   **sapiēns**, *wise.*
  equester, *of cavalry.*   **vetus**, *ancient.*

Decline together the following: —

  vir sapiēns, *a wise man.*   **vīta brevis**, *a short life.*
  ira praeceps, *headlong wrath.*   **ager pauper**, *a poor field.*
  rex potens, *a powerful king.*   **exsul inops**, *a destitute exile.*
  terra palūstris, *marsky land.*   **proelium ācre**, *a fierce battle.*

Translate into English.

1. Fortes fortuna juvat. 2. Sunt mitia poma, castaneae molles, et pressi copia lactis. 3. Milites proelio equestri pugnant. 4. Pauperes cum divitibus certant. 5. Viri fortes pericula non timent. 6. Triste remedium doloris ira est. 7. Non omnis via brevis

est facilis. 8. Jovis omnia plena sunt. 9. Custos es pauperis horti. 10. Sole sub ardenti resonant arbusta cicadis. 11. Regem infernum terret cum conjuge lumen. 12. Silvae cum montibus ardent. 13. Pecori. frondes, alimentaque mitia fruges humano generi, deis quoque tura ministrat tellus. 14. Atlas vix humeris candentem sustinet axem. 15. Phoebus equos amentes stimulo domat. 16. Di omnes deaeque Solem supplice voce rogant. 17. Julium sidus micat inter omnes velut luna inter minores ignes.

Write in Latin.

1. The mind of man is rich, not his chest. 2. Not every gathering of wild and barbarous [*men*] is a State. 3. All virtues are equal, and all vices are also equal: so the Stoics maintain. 4. Flattery is a fault of inconstant and deceitful men.

Lesson II.

Comparison of Adjectives.

1. Learn the regular forms of Comparison in § **17**, 1, with *a* and *b;* and compare the following: —

cārus, levis, fēlix, hebes, miser, celer, fēlix, ūber, vetus, facilis, similis, humilis.

2. Learn the forms of Irregular and Defective Comparison, § **17**, 2, 3, (with *a*); and compare the following: —

bonus, magnus, malus, multum, parvus, prior, propior, inferus, superus.

3. Decline together also the following, — forming the comparative or superlative according to the rules or examples given: —

vir bonus, *a better man.*   filius parvus (3.*b*), *the younger son.*
cōpia magnus, *the greatest forces.*   pugna ācer, *a very fierce fight.*
mos vetus, *a most ancient custom.*   nox longa, *the longest night.*
jūdex mitis, *a gentle judge.*   carmen jūcundus, *a jollier song.*

4. Learn the regular comparison of Adverbs, § 17, 4. Compare adverbs from the following:—

altus, *high.*   fortis, *brave.*   sapiēns, *wise.*
miser, *wretched.*   audāx, *bold.*   malus, *bad.*

Translate into English.

1. Hominum est infinita multitudo in Britannia, creberrimaque aedificia, fere Gallicis consimilia. Loca sunt temperatiora quam in Gallia, remissioribus frigoribus; noctes breviores quam in continenti. 2. Suevorum gens est longa maxima et bellicosissima Germanorum omnium: centum pagos habent; quotannis singula milia sunt in armis. 3. Unius urbis omnium pulcherrimae atque ornatissimae, Syracusarum, direptionem commemoro. Ex quattuor urbibus maximis constat. Una est *Insula;* et in insula extrema[1] fons aquae dulcis incredibili magnitudine,[2] plenissimus piscium. In altera urbe, *Achradina*, forum maximum, pulcherrimae porticus,[3] ornatissimum prytanium, amplissima est curia templumque egregium Jovis Olympii. In tertia, *Tycha* nominata, gymnasium amplissimum est et complures aedes sacrae. In quarta (*Neapoli* nominata, quia postrema aedificata) theatrum maximum; praeterea duo templa sunt egregia, Cereris unum, alterum Liberae; signumque Apollinis pulcherrimum et maximum.

[1] § 47, 8.   [2] See § 54, 7; G. 402.   [3] See the next Lesson.

Write in Latin.

1. The most healthful of all winds is the North wind. By night the Southeast-wind, by day the North-wind is more violent. 2. Of the gods the Gauls worship Mercury most. 3. They endure everything more easily than delay. 4. This is a very ancient custom. 5. Near the border of the ocean is the last point of the Ethiopians, where mightiest Atlas whirls the axle on his shoulder.

Lesson 12.

Fourth and Fifth Declensions.

1. *Fourth Declension.*—Learn § **12**, with 1, 2, and *d, e.* Decline the examples, giving the stem and meaning of each; decline together the following:—

1. **cantus dulcis**; 2. **domus excelsa**; 3. **cornū plēnum**; 4. **myrtus sacra**; 5. **manus valida**; 6. **portus tūtus**; 7. **īdūs Martiae**; 8. **vultus tristis.**

a. What is the stem of **domō**? of **domuī**? of **domī**? what is the meaning of the last?

b. What nouns of the fourth declension are feminine (2. *a*)? Which are neuter (2. *b*)?

c. What nouns have the dative and ablative plural in -**ubus**?

2. *Fifth Declension.*—Learn § **13**, with 1 and 2; and decline together the following:—

1. **rēs angusta**; 2. **tertius diēs**; 3. **speciēs honestior**.

What is the dative singular of **spēs**? the ablative of **diēs**? the accusative plural of **faciēs**? the genitive singular of **meridiēs**?

Translate into English.

1. Vultum tristem ostentat. 2. Hieme breviores sunt dies, aestate longiores. 3. Myrtus sacras manibus portant. 4. In tutis portubus sunt naves nostrae. 5. Species honesta magnas culpas celat. 6. Materiem superat opus. 7. Nec spes libertatis erat nec cura peculî. 8. Nostri vigiles nocturni quartā vigiliā ad curas laboremque mortales vocant, diemque nuntiant cantu; ipsum vero cantum plausu laterum.

Write in Latin.

1. The prisoner hides a glad hope with a sad countenance. 2. Foreign nations fear the decrees of the Roman Senate. 3. Sweet songs of Sirens charm the ear of Ulysses. 4. On the fourth day (*abl.*) before the Ides of March he calls a meeting of the conspirators at his own (*suae*) house.

Lesson 13.

Pronouns: Personal and Demonstrative.

Learn § **19**, 1, 2, 3, with *a;* also **20**, 1, 2, and decline the examples.

Observe that the inflection of these words includes several forms occurring in alius, ullus, etc. (Lesson 5, 3).

NOTE. — 1. The personal or demonstrative pronouns are in general used only for the sake of distinction or emphasis: as,

te voco, *I call you;* but
quis me vocat? ego te voco: *who calls me? it is I.*

2. The personal pronouns have the same construction as nouns, and their syntax in no respect differs from that of nouns.

3. The demonstrative pronouns are properly adjectives, and generally have a noun in agreement with them, either expressed or understood. But *in the oblique cases* they are often — especially **is** — used as personal pronouns of the third person: as,

Ti. Gracchus et frāter ējus Gāius tribunī plēbis erānt, *Tiberius Gracchus and his brother Caius were tribunes of the people.*

[For the special uses of the demonstratives, study § 20, 2. *a–e*.]

Translate into English.

1. Haec via nobis semper patet. 2. Senectus ipsa est morbus. 3. Scilicet res ipsa aspera est, sed vos non timetis eam. 4. Illa urbis pars tuta erat. 5. Hic plus venustatis, ille plus virium habet. 6. Mors nobis semper impendet. 7. Nemo nostrum immemor est vestri.[1] 8. Egomet me laudo. 9. Sibimet ipse arat agricola atque posteris suis. 10. Siculi auxilium sibi per me a vobis atque a populi Romani legibus orant. 11. Te tua carmina, me mea delectant. 12. Vigilantiam tuam tu mihi narras? 13. Hujus rei potestas omnis in vobis sita est, judices; totam rem publicam vos in hac causa tenetis, vos gubernatis.

[1] The genitive form in **um** is used as the *partitive*, that in **i** as the *objective* genitive (§ 50, 2, 3.)

Write in Latin.

1. You (emph.) carry in your right hand [*your*] liberty and fatherland. 2. You, Servius Tullius, reign by the will and consent of the citizens. 3. You are a foreigner; I a free citizen. 4. Physicians rarely treat themselves. 5. Now at last we please ourselves. 6. You have a leader mindful of you, forgetful of himself. 7. No one of us has the [*physical*] strength of Milo. 8. You were a sharer with me of those dangers.

Lesson 14.

Pronouns: Relative, Interrogative, and Indefinite.

1. *Relative.* — Learn § 21, 1, with the inflection of the relative pronoun **qui**.

NOTE. — The forms **quis** (*who?* or *anyone*) and **quid** (*what?* or *any thing*) are never relatives. But all the forms of the relative pronoun are also interrogative and indefinite.

Learn § 48, and observe that —

1. Every relative implies some demonstrative word (or antecedent) to which it refers.

2. A sentence containing a relative *must have at least two verbs*, — one belonging to the relative. [Either of the verbs may, however, be understood.]

3. A relative pronoun is properly an Adjective, in agreement with some word either expressed in its own clause, or implied in the antecedent clause. This word is in Latin very frequently found in the relative clause, — sometimes in that alone, — though rarely or never in English: as,

erant duo itinera quibus itineribus domō exīre possent, *there were two ways by which* [ways] *they could go out from home*.

[See examples in § 48, 3. *a, b, c.*]

4. The relative clause in Latin oftener stands before the demonstrative (or antecedent) clause, while in English it more usually follows.

2. *Interrogative.* — Learn the inflection of the Interrogatives —

quis, quī, with **quisnam, ecquis, numquis.**

NOTE. — Notice the difference in use between **quis** and **qui,** etc. (see *a*). **Quisnam** is emphatic, *pray, who?* **Ecquis** and **numquis** are compounded from the indefinite and the interrogative particle, **en** and **num**; and mean not *who?* but *any* (see 2. *d*): as,

ecquis nos videt? *does any one see us?*
numquid hoc dubitās? *do you at all doubt this?*

3. *Indefinite.* — Learn the inflection of the following (2. *c, d, e*) : —

quīdam, *a certain one.*	**quisquam,** *any one* (2, *b*).
quīvīs, *any one.*	**aliquis,** *some one.*
quisque, *every one.*	**quis,** *one.*
unusquisque, *each.*	**siquis,** *if any.*

All these are construed either as simple adjectives or as nouns. But notice the difference in the use of **quis** and **qui** in these compounds (1, *c*).

Learn 2, *a*, with the inflection of **quisquis** (2. *b*).

NOTE. — The indefinite relative — in English *whoever, whatever* — is in construction a true relative, of which, however, the antecedent is very rarely expressed. Observe that it is regularly formed in Latin in two ways : 1. by adding **-cumque** (**-cunque**) to the *relative;* 2. by doubling the *interrogative.*

[Compare the forms **ubicumque** or **ubiubi,** etc., in § 22.]

4. *Correlative.* — Learn § 21, 2. *g*, and § 22, so as to know the correspondence of the relative and demonstrative forms. Observe that —

1. With the exception of **quando** (*when?*) the relative and interrogative forms are alike throughout.

2. The relative Adverbs — as **cum,** *when;* **ubi,** *where;* **quō,** *whither;* **unde,** *whence* — follow the same rules of construction as relative Pronouns.

Translate into English.

1. Insula naturā triquetra, cujus unum latus est contra Galliam. Hujus lateris alter angulus (qui est ad Cantium) ad orientem solem, inferior ad meridiem

spectat. Materia cujusque generis ut in Gallia est, praeter fagum atque abietem. 2. Est in Hercynia silva bos cervi figurā,[1] cujus a media fronte inter aures unum cornu exstat. 3. Sed quis hic est homo, quem ante aedes video? non placet. 4. Quo ambulas tu, qui volcanum in cornu conclusum habes? 5. Quis herus est tibi? Amphitruo, quicum nupta est Alcumena. 6. Sed cum cogito, equidem certo idem sum qui semper eram. 7. 'Studes'? 'Etiam.' 'Ubi'? 'Mediolani.' 'Cur non hic'? 'Quia nullos hic praeceptores habemus.' 8. Illi falsi sunt, qui diversas res pariter exspectant, ignaviae voluptatem, et praemia virtutis. 9. Alia omnia vasta [erant], inculta, egentia aquae, infesta serpentibus, quarum vis, sic uti omnium ferarum, inopiā cibi acrior [est]. 10. Portat maniplos, unde *maniplaris* nomen miles habet. 11. Quilibet hic tutus est. 12. Quicumque nefas audent, morte jacent merita. Testes estis, Philippi, quorum sparsis ossibus albet humus. 13. Quot homines, tot sententiae. 14. Tale tuum carmen [est], divine poëta, quale sopor fessis in gramine. 15. Quo[2] quisque est sollertior et ingeniosior, hoc docet iracundius et laboriosius. 16. Neque ex castris Catilinae quisquam omnium transfuga erat.

[1] Translate by OF (§ 54, 7).   [2] See § 22, c.

Write in Latin.

1. Whatever is conspicuous among [*its*] neighbors is great there where it is conspicuous. For greatness has an uncertain measure. A ship which is large in a river is small in the sea. A helm which is large for one ship is small for another. 2. As other good things, so every good book is better, the larger [*it is*]. 3. I have frequent discussion with a certain learned man, to whom nothing is so pleasing as brevity.

Lesson 15.

Numerals.

1. Learn § **18**, 1, with the list of Cardinal Numbers, and the declension of those which are declinable (*a*, *b*, *c*, *d*, *e*).

2. Learn the method of forming the Ordinals, Distributives, and Numeral Adverbs; and commit to memory the exceptional ones (1 to 5).

a. The cardinal numbers are constantly used in denoting *measures of time and space*. In such expressions the accusative is generally used to denote duration of time or extent of space; but sometimes the genitive (of quality, § **55**, 2. *a*) is used with nouns.

b. To express miles, the phrase **milia passuum** is used; one thousand *passus*, or *paces*, being the length of the Roman mile.

c. Give in Latin the following numbers:—

13, 58, 87, 45, 120, 625, 1560, 1874, 25,000, 1,000,000; 5th, 25th, 125th; once; twice; 5 times; 25 times; 10 apiece.

Translate into English.

1. Mille meae Siculis errant in montibus agnae. 2. Bis senos quotannis nostra dies altaria fumant. 3. A lacu Lemanno ad montem Juram, milia passuum decem novem, murus in altitudinem pedum sedecim fossaque erant. 4. Tertiā fere vigiliā castra movet. 5. Reliqua sunt tritici trecenta viginti quatuor milia modiûm.[1] 6. Olympiade centesima quarta decima Lysippus erat. 7. Tullus regnat annos duos et triginta.

[1] See § **10**, 4. *e.*

Write in Latin.

1. I see an army of ten thousand soldiers on [*their*] march. 2. One hundred and twenty-five men are in the citadel. 3. He gives to his [*men*] two horses [*each*]. 4. The army has two camps. 5. Cæsar was proconsul in Gaul twice five years (2, *c*). 6. We have a flock of six hundred sheep.

Lesson 16.

Verb-Forms.

1. Learn the whole of § **23**, 1, 2, with § **24**, and *read* the Notes.
2. Learn § **27**, 1, 4, 5. *a*, *b*, *c*; § **28**, 1 (*read a*, *b*, *c*), 2 (*read* the sections *a* to *h*).

Questions on the above.

1. What are the Moods of a Latin verb? What Tenses are wanting in the Subjunctive? in the Imperative? Which are the compound tenses of the Passive (2. *b*)? how are they formed?
2. How is the Indicative Mood used? the Subjunctive? the Imperative? the Infinitive?
3. Which are the tenses of *incomplete* (or *continued*) action? of *completed* action? How are the latter formed in the Passive?
4. Upon what stem are the tenses of incomplete action formed? those of completed action? the perfect participle?
5. What are the Personal Endings of the active voice? of the passive? What changes are made in the verb-stem? What is the formation of the so-called supine stem (§ **28**, 2. *f*)?

N. B. The learner is advised to study the forms given in the Table on page 56, and to keep them before his eye, in his reading of Latin sentences, until they are quite familiar. The four regular conjugations simply have these forms either in combination with the characteristic vowel or modified by it (§ **30**).

Lesson 17.

The Verb ESSE, *to be*.

1. Learn § **29**, with the Principal Parts and the full Conjugation of **esse**, giving the meaning of each form in English; also *a* and *b*.

a. Notice the division of the tenses into two groups, — one (the tenses of *continued action*) being formed from the root ES, found in the English *am, is;* the other (the tenses of *completed action*) being formed from the root FU, found in the English *be*. By noticing these different roots, with the tenses formed from each, the learner will be guided in distinguishing the corresponding formations in other verbs, where the stems only and not the roots differ.

b. Compare the inflection of **esse** with the table of verb-endings given on page 56. It will be noticed that the imperfect and future differ from the forms in **-bam** and **-bo**, which are compound forms; and that these tenses of **esse** are used in forming the regular terminations of the pluperfect and future perfect: as, **fu-eram, fu-ero**. These terminations, with all those formed upon the perfect stem, *are alike for all verbs in the language*, whether regular or irregular.

c. The Principal Parts (given at the head) should always be carefully committed to memory, as in these are found the different stems on which the several groups of tenses are formed (§ 30, 5).

2. Give the mood, tense, &c., with the meaning, of the following: —

1. fuistī; 2. eritis; 3. fuissem; 4. essēmus; 5. fuerātis; 6. fuisse; 7. fuerim; 8. sīnt; 9. fore; 10. forēnt; 11. esse; 12. essētis; 13. futūrum esse; 14. fuerimus; 15. potuit; 16. possēnt; 17. possint; 18. prōdestis; 19. potuisse; 20. potuisset; 21. esto; 22. sunto; 23. fuērunt; 24. erimus; 25. fuerit; 26. prōderit; 27. prōsīmus; 28. potuerit.

Lesson 18.

Moods and Tenses,

Review § **24**; learn §§ **25**, 1, 2, 3, 4; **26**, 1, 2; **27**, 1, 2, 3, 4.

Questions on the above.

1. What are the chief uses of the Subjunctive? Express in Latin the words *I may write; I can write; I would write.* Give the English of the following: —

eāmus; adsum ut videam; imperat ut scrībam; vereor nē eat; sunt qui putēnt.

2. What is the termination of the present participle (**-ns**)? its meaning? Of the future participle (**-turus**)? its meaning and use? Of the perfect participle (**-tus** or **-sus**)? Of the Gerundive (**-dus**)? its adjective meaning? its use in the oblique cases?

3. What is the Gerund form? its meaning? What is the Supine? how is it to be translated?

4. Which are the tenses of incomplete (continued) action? of completed action? of indefinite action?

5. What distinction in meaning between the imperfect and the perfect? Give examples. What are the two uses of the perfect? Give an example of the perfect *definite;* of the perfect *historical.* Translate the words **longius prosequī vetuit, quod locī nātūram ignōrābat;** and point out the use of the tenses.

6. How are the tenses of completed action formed in the passive? Express in Latin, *Cæsar was slain; he had been slain.*

Lesson 19.

Regular Verb: First Conjugation.
I. ACTIVE VOICE.

Learn § 30, with 1. *a, b, c;* and compare § 28, 2. *f,* with Note.

a. Inflect the Active Voice of **amo** (§ 31) as far as and including the Imperative Mood; giving first the Principal Parts and the Synopsis (§ 30, 5. *a, b*).

b. Compare the inflection with that of **esse,** noticing the two stems (present and perfect) corresponding to the two roots ES and FU (§ 27, 5. *a, b*).

c. Compare the inflection of **amo** with the Personal Endings in § 28, 1. *a, b, c;* also 2. *c.*

d. Like **amo** inflect the following:—

aro, *plough.*   paro. *prepare.*   spēro, *hope.*
creo, *create, appoint.*   pugno, *fight.*   voco, *call.*

e. Learn (from the list on page 67) the Principal Parts, and give the full Synopsis of the following:—

do, *give.*   juvo, *help, please.*   sto, *stand.*
domo, *subdue.*   seco, *cut.*   veto, *forbid.*

f. Describe the following forms:—

1. arābit; 2. amāverat (or amārat, § 30, 6, *a*); 3. dedit; 4. parāvisset (parāsset); 5. stetērunt; 6. jūverint; 7. spērāvistī (spērāstī); 8. domuissent; 9. secuerat; 10. domābant; 11. vetuistis; 12. dedēre; 13. paret; 14. juvārent; 15. pugnābis; 16. dāto; 17. vocānto; 18. secuerim; 19. vocābitis.

Translate into English.

1. Pausanias non mores patrios solum, sed etiam cultum vestitumque mutavit. Idem magnam belli gloriam turpi morte maculavit. 2. Dionis mors mirabiliter vulgi mutavit voluntatem. Nam qui vivum eum tyrannum vocaverant, idem liberatorem patriae tyrannique expulsorem praedicabant. 3. Non omnes arbusta juvant humilesque myricae. 4. Durus agricola nudus arato. 5. Pugna tecum ipse. 6. Jamque faces et arma volant; furor arma ministrat. 7. Populus Romanus M. Tullium Ciceronem consulem[1] creavit. 8. Revocate animos: durate, et vosmet rebus servate secundis. 9. Liberemus diuturnā curā populum Romanum.

[1] § 46, 2, third example.

Write in Latin.

1. The sword gave to Cato the liberty which it could not to his country. 2. Ennius compares his own[1] [*old age*] to the old age of a spirited and victorious horse. 3. I shall often praise that sage Bias. He did not think these playthings of fortune even his own [*property*] which we even call blessings. 4. Let us sing the new trophies of Augustus.

[1] Notice that (contrary to the English idiom) Ellipsis is more likely to occur in the first than the second of a pair of ideas.

Lesson 20.

Regular Verb: First Conjugation.

2. PASSIVE VOICE.

Learn the forms of the Passive Voice of **amo**, corresponding with those already given in the Active.

Compare the *personal endings* of the active and passive (§ 28, 1); see also the signification of the passive form as given in the Note.

First Conjugation.

Observe that —

1. In the tenses of *completed action* in the passive, — the perfect, pluperfect, and future perfect, — the participle (**amātus**, &c.) is treated as an adjective, agreeing in gender and number with the subject of the verb: as,

 bellum parātum est, *war has been prepared.*
 Gallī domitī erānt, *the Gauls had been subdued.*
 nāvēs dēpressae sunt, *the ships were sunk.*

2. The passive construction is an inversion of the active, in which the object of the action becomes subject, while the subject (or agent) takes a dependent form, as follows —

a. If the agent is a person, or treated as a person (personified), it is put in the ablative with the preposition **a** or **ab**, BY: as,

 Caesar domuit Gallōs, *Cæsar subdued the Gauls;*
 Gallī a Caesare domitī sunt, *the Gauls were subdued by Cæsar.*

b. If not a person, it is put in the ablative alone, or in the accusative with **per**: as,

 famēs necat hominēs, *hunger destroys men;*
 hominēs famē necāntur, *men are destroyed by hunger.*

3. An Intransitive verb (having no immediate object) cannot strictly be made passive. But in Latin such verbs are used *impersonally*, in the third person singular only: as,

 pugnātum est, *there was fighting;* lit. *it* [a battle] *was fought.*

Describe the following forms: —

1. arātūr; 2. amāminī; 3. pugnātum erit; 4. creābātur; 5. domitī essent; 6. secta erānt; 7. vocāberis; 8. parārētur; 9. vetitum erat; 10. domitī essent; 11. vocābuntur; 12. regnāntō; 13. vocābere; 14. dētūr; 15. paratī sint.

Translate into English.

1. Alesia, urbs Gallica nobilis, a Caesare oppugnata est. 2. Cicero a populo Romano consul creatus est. 3. Hic jam ter centum totos regnabitur annos, donec regina sacerdos geminam dabit prolem. 4. Libertas nostra fortiter vindicata est. 5. Ego M. Regulum nec infelicem nec miserum unquam putavi; non enim magnitudo animi cruciabatur ejus a Poenis, non denique animus ipse. 6. O domus antiqua, heu

quam dispari dominare domino! 7. Tempora mutantur (§ 23, 3), et nos mutamur in illis.

Write in Latin.

1. Gold is proved by fire, brave men by misery. 2. From an appearance of advantage wrong-is-done very often in politics. 3. They fought very bravely and hotly on-both-sides. 4. Mithridates had got together a very large force (plur.). 5. The most fertile regions of Germany had-been-taken-possession-of by the Suevi.

Lesson 21.

Regular Verb: First Conjugation.
3. NOUN AND ADJECTIVE FORMS.

1. *Noun Forms.* — Learn the Infinitive Mood of **amo** in both voices, with §§ 57, 8; 58, 11; also the Gerund and Supine, with § 25.

a. The Infinitive is used (as in English) with verbs where the sense would be incomplete without another action *of the same subject* (*Complementary infinitive,* § 57, 8. *c*): as,

consilia non possum mūtāre, *I cannot change* [*my*] *plans.*
Such verbs are *to be able, to dare, to begin* or *cease,* and the like.

b. The infinitive is used *like the nominative of a neuter noun* in such sentences as —

humānum est errāre, *to err is human.*

c. It is used *like the accusative of a neuter noun* in such sentences as —

hostēs parānt expugnāre oppidum, *the enemy prepare to storm the town.*

d. In either of these uses, it may take as subject the accusative of a noun or pronoun: as,

senem saltāre indecōrum est, *for an old man to dance is unbecoming.*

video tē claudum esse, *I see that you are lame.*
Here the object of **video,** i. e. the thing seen, is really the substantive clause **te esse claudum,** not the simple accusative **te.**

e. The infinitive with a subject-accusative is most commonly used as the object of verbs of *knowing, thinking,* or *telling* (§ 57, 8. *e*). Used in this way, it becomes the principal verb in INDIRECT DISCOURSE (§ 67, 1).

f. The Gerund is used *in the oblique cases* as a participial noun, of which the infinitive serves as nominative or accusative (as in *b, c,* above): as,

multae sunt causae peccāndī, *many are the motives for sinning.*

g. The Supine is a noun of the fourth declension in the accusative and ablative cases, but having only special uses (see § 74). It may always be translated by the English Infinitive.

2. *Adjective Forms.* — Learn the Participles of **amo**, active and passive, with § **72**, 1, 2. *a, b, c,* and 3.

[For the inflection of the Participles, see § **16**, 1, and 3. *a.*]

a. Participles correspond in meaning to English Participles and govern the same cases as their verbs. They may all be used also as simple adjectives, and the present and perfect are even sometimes compared as adjectives.

b. The Gerundive *in the oblique cases* has peculiar constructions to be shown hereafter.

c. The future participle in -**rus** is translated by "*going to,*" "*about to,*" or "*to:*" as, **ventūra sēcula,** *ages to come.*

d. The Perfect Participle is most frequently used with the tenses of **esse** in forming the *tenses of completed action* in the passive.

e. The Future Participle and the Gerundive are often used with the tenses of **esse**, to make what are sometimes called the *first and second periphrastic conjugations* (see and learn § **40**, *a* and *b*).

f. The Participle in -**dus** regularly, and the Perfect Participle often, have the personal agent in the DATIVE instead of the ablative with **a** or **ab**.

[Observe that the participle in -**rus** is always ACTIVE, the participle in -**dus** always PASSIVE].

Translate into English.

1. Numquam est utile peccare. 2. Non potest artifex mutare materiam. 3. Lex Papiria vetat aedīs injussu plebis consecrari. 4. Te hilari animo[1] esse et prompto ad jocandum valde me juvat. 5. Te ipsum

nunc et[2] animi quodam impetu concitatum et[2] recentibus praeceptorum studiis flagrantem jam aetas mitigabit. 6. In ea re per L. Caecilium Sulla accusatur, in qua re est uterque laudandus. 7. Multo maxima pars eorum qui in tabernis sunt, immo vero genus hoc universum amantissimum est otii. 8. Habetis consulem ex plurimis periculis et insidiis atque ex media morte non ad vitam suam sed ad salutem vestram reservatum. 9. De vestra vita, de conjugum vestrarum atque liberorum anima, de fortunis omnium, hodierno die vobis judicandum est.

[1] See § 54, 7. [2] Correlative.

Write in Latin.

1. Our powers must be compared with the things which we are going-to-attempt. 2. Better is a sure peace than a hoped-for victory. 3. It is advantageous to give attention to letters. 4. Galba, denying nothing in his own behalf and imploring the protection of the Roman people, commended [to them] both his own children and the son of Caius Gallus.

Lesson 22.

Regular Verb: Second Conjugation.

1. Learn § 30, 2; with *a, b, c, d, e.*

a. Inflect **moneo** (§ 32) in both voices, comparing its forms with those of **amo**. (Notice that the difference is almost entirely in *the vowel of conjugation,* or *characteristic vowel;* in the present subjunctive, however, another vowel is added.)

b. Give the Synopsis, both by moods and by stems; with the Participles and Infinitives.

c. In like manner inflect the following: —

    habeo, *have.*   terreo, *alarm.*

Also the following, which have no Supine: —

    lateo, *lie hid.*   timeo, *fear.*
    pateo, *be open.*   pareo, *obey.*

2. Learn (from the list on page 69) the Principal Parts, and give the full synopsis of the following:—

deleo, *destroy.* maneo, *remain.* sedeo, *sit.*
doceo, *teach.* mordeo, *bite.* teneo, *hold.*
jubeo, *command.* moveo, *move.* video, *see.*
lūceo, *shine.* rīdeo, *laugh.* voveo, *vow.*

Describe the following forms:—

1. monuerat; 2. tenēbitur; 3. mōtus est; 4. sedēbimus; 5. manserāmus; 6. momorderat; 7. respondistis; 8. docueritis; 9. paruerānt; 10. sēdit; 11. mansissent; 12. latuistī; 13. vidērunt; 14. vīsus es; 15. doctī sunt.

Translate into English.

1. Sta, miles, hic optime manebimus. 2. Caesar castra moverat. 3. Omnes artes quae ad humanitatem pertinent habent quoddam commune vinculum et quasi cognatione quadam inter se continentur. 4. Bis consul fuerat P. Africanus et duos terrores hujus imperi Karthaginem Numantiamque deleverat cum accusavit L. Cottam. 5. Aedem voverat L. Aemilius. 6. Delenda est Karthago. 7. Suis flammis delete Fidenas. 8. Magnus motus servilis eo anno in Apulia fuit. Tarentum provinciam L. Postumus habebat. Is de pastorum conjuratione, qui vias latrociniis pascuaque publica infesta habuerant, quaestionem severe exercuit. Ad septem milia hominum condemnavit. 9. Palus erat non magna inter nostrum et hostium exercitum. Intra eas silvas hostes in occulto sese continebant; in aperto loco secundum flumen paucae stationes equitum videbantur.

Write in Latin.

1. He held in (*his*) hand a sword. 2. The Sabine women were weeping. 3. We were alarmed by the sound of arms. 4. I have replied to the most serious charges. 5. The soldiers, to whom the king was very dear, for some time maintained a mournful silence.

Lesson 23.

Regular Verb: Third Conjugation.

1. Learn § **30**, 3, with *a* to *h*, reading carefully the points numbered from 1 to 8 (*a*), and 1 to 5 (*b*).

a. Inflect **rego** and **capio** (§ 33) in both voices, giving the Principal Parts and the synopsis by moods and stems.

b. Notice especially the parts marked by the characteristic vowel, as the infinitive and imperative with the imperfect subjunctive in the active voice, and the present indicative in the passive; and compare the future indicative with the corresponding form in the first and second conjugations, and with the present subjunctive.

2. Learn (from the list on pages 72, 73) the Principal Parts, and give the full synopsis of the following, explaining the formation of the several stems from the root: —

cado, *fall.*	frango, *break.*	tendo, *stretch.*
caedo, *cut.*	gigno, *produce.*	texo, *weave.*
cano, *sing.*	laedo, *hurt.*	vinco, *conquer.*
cēdo, *yield.*	nosco, *know.*	cupio, *desire.*
dīco, *say.*	scrībo, *write.*	facio, *make.*
disco, *learn.*	tango, *touch.*	jacio, *throw.*
fallo, *deceive.*	tego, *cover.*	rapio, *seize.*

a. In the verbs in **io**, observe that the stem-vowel (ĭ) disappears before ĕ or ĭ (short), except in the future third singular (capiet), where the e was originally long. Note also that **facio** has no passive forms from the present stem (§ **37**, 7).

b. Describe the following forms: —
1. fēcerānt; 2. cecidisset; 3. cēssērunt; 4. scripsimus; 5. jacta sunt; 6. tetigisset; 7. laesī erānt; 8. factum est; 9. frēgit; 10. rapiēmus; 11. faciāmus; 12. faciēbānt; 13. cupierat (cupīverat); 14. discit; 15. dīxero; 16. dīcitis; 17. didicero; 18. dīxistis; 19. tectus esset; 20. tactus esset; 21. textus esset; 22. vīcerāmus; 23. vixerāmus; 24. rapiēnt; 25. pepigisset.

Translate into English.

1. Magno fragore arbor cecidit. 2. Ferrea securi arborem cecīdit. 3. Exercitum suum in Italiam

duxit Hannibal. 4. Magna clade Romani Cannis victi sunt. 5. Jacta est alea. 6. Rem acu tetigisti. 7. Pyrrhi temporibus jam Apollo versus facere desierat. 8. Emito agrum cum jacent pretia praediorum. 9. Quattuor tragoedias sedecim diebus absolvisti. 10. Hannibal imperator factus proximo triennio omnes gentes Hispaniae bello subegit. 11. Summis suppliciis fures afficiuntor. 12. Hoc tempore obsequium amicos, veritas odium parit. 13. Murus Babylonis coctili laterculo structus erat. 14. Mihi quidem Scipio quamquam est subito ereptus, vivit tamen semperque vivet. Virtutem enim amavi illius viri, quae exstincta non est. 15. Saepe rixam conclamatum in vicino incendium solvit.

Write in Latin.

1. Caesar had led (his) army into Gaul. 2. Labor conquers all things. 3. I have received two letters from you dated at Corcyra. 4. I wrote thirteen letters in one day. 5. Hannibal conquered the Roman army at Cannae. 6. Codrus, king of the Athenians, laid aside his royal apparel, put on a shepherd's garb, and stirring up a quarrel was slain. 7. We learn by teaching.

Lesson 24.

Regular Verb: Fourth Conjugation.

1. Learn § **30**, 4, with *a, b, c, d;* also 5. *a,* observing that in the tenses of the perfect stem (except the perfect itself) **v** is almost always omitted in verbs of this conjugation.

a. Inflect **audio** (§ 34) in both voices, giving the Principal Parts and the Synopsis by moods and stems.

b. Notice especially the parts marked by the characteristic vowel (compare Lesson 23); and the general similarity between this and the third conjugation, corresponding with that between the first and second.

c. Like **audio** inflect the following: —
    fīnio, *finish.*   mūnio, *fortify.*   scio, *know.*

2. Learn (from the list on page 75) the Principal Parts and give the full synopsis of the following: —
    aperio, *open.*   sentio, *feel.*   venio, *come.*
    reperio, *find.*   sepelio, *bury.*   vincio, *bind.*

Describe the following forms: —

1. audierat; 2. sensērunt; 3. vēnissem; 4. reperītur; 5. sepultī sunt; 6. aperuit portam; 7. vinctus erit; 8. ventum erat; 9. urbem munīvit; 10. sciēbat; 11. vēnerānt; 12. fīnītum est; 13. repererānt; 14. ventum erat; 15. scīsset; 16. vīcerimus; 17. vīxerimus; 18. vīnxerimus.

Translate into English.

1. Non omnia scimus. 2. Urbs muris validis munita erat. 3. Haud facile aurum reperitur. 4. Aedis portam aperuit. 5. Ferreis catenis servum vinxere. 6. Themistocli ad nostram memoriam monumenta manserunt duo, sepulcrum prope oppidum in quo est sepultus, statuae in foro Magnesiae. 7. Crepitum armorum paene audimus. 8. Aedes Minervae est in insula quam Marcellus non attigit, quam plenam et ornatam reliquit. Pugna erat equestris Agathocli regis, in tabulis picta. His autem tabulis interiores templi parietes vestiebantur.

Write in Latin.

1. I came, saw, conquered. 2. The camp was fortified with a strong rampart. 3. Guards, open the gates. 4. He bound the prisoners with three chains (each). 5. We heard the crash of a falling tree. 6. The noise of arms was no longer heard. 7. Sicily is bounded on all sides by the sea. 8. Whatever has reached [*its*] highest is near [*its*] end.

Lesson 25.

Deponent Verbs.

1. Learn § 35, 1, with *a*, *b*, *c*, *d*, and 2; giving in full the Principal Parts and Synopsis of all the examples (see § 30, 6. *a*, *b*, *c*).

2. Give the synopsis of the following, consulting the list in 1. *h*: —

moror, *delay*.
hortor, *encourage*.
experior, *try*.
fateor, *confess*.
loquor, *speak*.

morior, *die*.
patior, *suffer*.
proficiscor, *set out*.
queror, *complain*.
ūtor, *use*.

NOTE. — The future infinitive of Deponents is always to be given in the *active form:* thus of sequor it is secūtūrus esse, not secūtum iri.

a. Observe that the conjugation of the present stem is determined by the Infinitive, which corresponds to the passive infinitive of the four conjugations (§ 28, 2. *g*); while the rest of the forms are shown by the participle. Thus, queror, querī, questus, is conjugated like the passive of the 3d conjugation; its supine stem being quest-.

b. The passive originally expressed an action *done to one's self*, or in some way returning upon the subject. The deponents retained the active meaning, though the reflexive idea was in a great measure lost. It may, however, be still traced in many deponents. (Compare § 28, 1. note; also § 35, 1. *e*, *f*, *g*).

Translate into English.

1. Filius sequitur patrem, non passibus aequis. 2. Mox proficiscemur. 3. Polliciti sunt auxilium. 4. Non ausus est venire. 5. Naturae sollertiam nulla ars, nulla manus, nemo opifex consequi potest imitando. 6. Vir bonus non mentietur. 7. Romani veteres peregrinum regem aspernabantur. 8. Hortos egregiasque domos mercabitur. 9. Gladiator, morere fortiter. 10. Legatus militibus frumentum metietur.

11. Anatum ova gallinis saepe supponimus, e quibus pulli orti primum aluntur ab his ut a matribus, a quibus exclusi fotique sunt, deinde eas relinquunt et effugiunt sequentes, cum primum aquam quasi naturalem domum videre potuerunt. 12. Tum vero ferrea proles exorta est, ausaque funestum fabricari ensem.

Write in Latin.

1. He set out from the camp on the third day. 2. We have confessed our fault. 3. He spoke much, but not many [*things*]. 4. The Roman people suffered many great disasters. 5. I tried a doubtful remedy. 6. The daughter followed [*her*] father's footsteps.

Lesson 26.
Irregular, Defective, and Impersonal Verbs.

1. *Irregular.* — Learn §. 37, and inflect the examples; giving the principal parts, the synopsis (with the participles), and the full inflection of the present tense in all the moods.

Observe that all the irregularities occur in the first or present stem, and consist mostly in the absence of any vowel of conjugation.

2. *Defective.* — Learn § 38, 1. *a, b, c;* and 2, with *a* to *h*, so far as to recognize the forms.

3. *Impersonal.* — Learn § 39, and read carefully *a, b, c, d*, giving the full synopsis (in the third person singular, with infinitives and gerund) of the verbs in *b* and *d*.

a. Notice that these verbs are conjugated like others of similar endings (those in -at as verbs of the 1st conjugation, and those in -et as those of the 2d, etc.): as **oportet, oportēbat, oportuit, oportēre**.

b. The verbs in *b* have sometimes the *tenses of completed action* in the passive (deponent) form: as, **licuit** or **licitum est**, etc.

c. The verbs in *b* and *c* can rarely be translated literally, but must be rendered by a different idiom: as, **poenitet me**, *I repent* (*am sorry* or *dissatisfied*), etc.

Irregular and Impersonal Verbs.

4. Describe the following forms: —

1. vultis (voltis); 2. velim; 3. vellem; 4. nollet; 5. malim; 6. voluisse; 7. fert; 8. tulerat; 9. ferris; 10. fertor; 11. latī erant; 12. estur; 13. ībunt; 14. īvisset (īsset); 15. eāmus; 16. euntis; 17. fierī; 18. faxim; 19. fīunto; 20. factum est; 21. benefīat; 22. coeperānt; 23. coeptus est; 24. ōdērunt; 25. memento; 26. āiēbat; 27. inquit; 28. fāre; 29. quaesumus; 30. nequībunt; 31. infit; 32. grandinat; 33. nōs poenitēbit; 34. nōbīs eundum est; 35. licuisset; 36. juvābit; 37. praestābat; 38. interfuit; 39. pigeat; 40. licitum erat.

Translate into English.

1. Miles qui decimae legionis aquilam ferebat "Desilite" inquit "commilitones, nisi vultis aquilam hostibus prodere." Tum se ex navi projecit, atque in hostes aquilam ferre coepit. 2. Visne tu meminisse hominem te esse natum? 3. 'Quisquis homo huc profecto venerit pugnos edet.' 'Apage! non placet me hoc (*at this time*) noctis esse; cenavi modo.' 4. Auferere, non abibis, si ego fustem sumpsero. 5. Parva fuit, si prima velis elementa referre, Roma. 6. Licet occultos monitus audire deorum; certe fama licere putat. 7. Si modo credimus, unum isse diem sine sole ferunt. 8. Magnae pereunt cum moenibus urbes. 9. Sordidum me et incultis moribus [esse] aiunt; quod lubet confiteri, Quirites. 10. In victoria vel ignavis gloriari licet. 11. Res in senatu agitari coepta est. 12. Tandem fit surculus arbor.

Write in Latin.

1. The old age of those who are courted by the young is made less burdensome. 2. Go hence to your betrothed with your untimely love. So may every Roman [woman] go who mourns an enemy. 3. This is no friendship when one does not wish to hear the truth, the other is prepared to lie.

Lesson 27.

Formation of Verb-Stems.

Review § 30, 5, *a*; learn *c*, *d*.

Give the principal parts of the verbs which follow; explaining with the aid of the teacher the formation of the different stems from the root. Compare the appended derivatives from the same root.

N, B. The small figures 1, 2, 3, 4, represent the conjugations, and refer to the corresponding subsections of § 30. For euphonic changes, see § 1, 3. *a*, *b*, etc.

1. voco¹ (VOC), *call;* vōx, *voice.*
2. seco¹ (SEC), *cut;* segmentum, *slice.*
3. do¹ (DA), *give;* dōnum, *gift.*
4. cubo¹ (CUB), *lie;* cumbo (see below).
5. lūceo² (LUC), *shine;* lūcidus, *bright.*
6. augeo² (AUG), *increase;* augustus, *august.*
7. haereo² (HAES, simplest known form), *cling;* haesito, *hesitate.*
8. suādeo² (SVAD), *make pleasant;* suāvis, *sweet.*
9. video² (VID), *see;* visio, *sight.*
10. doceo² (DOC), *teach;* docilis, *teachable.*
11. mordeo² (MORD), *bite;* mordāx, *biting.*
12. cumbo³ (CUB, see cubo), *recline;* cubīle, *couch.*
13. cado³ (CAD), *fall;* cāsus, *accident.*
14. caedo³ (id.), *fell;* caedēs, *massacre.*
15. emo³ (EM), *buy;* emāx, *eager to purchase.*
16. sisto³ (STA), *stand* (compare sto, stāre).
17. gigno³ (GEN), *produce;* genus, *race.*
18. disco³ (DIC), *learn* (compare dico and doceo).
19. nosco³ (GNO), *know;* nōmen, *name.*
20. sterno³ (STAR), *strew;* strāmentum, *litter.*
21. alo³ (AL), *nourish;* almus, *benign.*
22. crē-do³ (DHA), *trust* (*place confidence*).
23. fīnio⁴ (from fīnī- stem of fīnis), *end.*
24. sentio⁴ (SENT), *perceive;* sententia, *opinion.*
25. salio⁴ (SAL), *leap;* salto, *dance.*
26. re-perio⁴ (PAR, compare pario), *find.*
27. nascor³ (GNA, compare GEN in gigno), *be born.*
28. nanciscor³ (NAC), *get;* compare pernix, *untiring.*
29. memini (MEN), *remember;* compare mens, *mind.*
30. eo (I), *go* (compare ven-eo, *to be sold*); iter, *way.*

Lesson 28.
Particles.

1. *Adverbs.* — Learn § 41, with 1, *a* and *b* (reading the subsections *d* to *l*), and 2 (classification of Adverbs).

The learner should commit to memory the first five groups of correlatives under 2, *a*; and notice the regularity of all.

2. *Prepositions.* — Learn §. 42, 1, with *a*, *b*, *c*, including the lists of Prepositions, with their meaning, and 3 (prepositions in Compounds).

N. B. If thought desirable, only the *more common* prepositions in *a* and *b* may be committed to memory, the teacher marking them in the list.

3. *Conjunctions.* — Learn § 43, 1, with *a* and *b* (classification of Conjunctions).

Questions on the above.

1. What parts of speech are Particles? 2. Why so called (see § 5, 4)? 3. Are these parts of speech always distinguished from one another? 4. How are Adverbs formed from adjectives of the first and second declensions? 5. How from adjectives of the third declension? 6. What cases of adjectives are regularly used as adverbs? 7. How do you explain the forms multum, falsō, contrā, citrā, ibi, deinde, statim, palam, forās, penitus, anteā, obviam, quamobrem, forsitan, scīlicet? 8. How are adverbs classified? Give an example of each class.

9. How are Prepositions distinguished from Adverbs? 10. Which prepositions require to be followed by the Accusative? 11. Which by the Ablative? 12. Which are followed by either case? 13. With what distinction in meaning, in the case of in and sub? 14. Which prepositions are most frequently used as adverbs (see § 56, 3, *d*)? 15. What is the adverbial meaning, in compounds, of the following: a (ab), ad, con, dē, in, ob?

16. Which classes of Conjunctions are coördinate? 17. Which are subordinate? 18. What is the meaning of those terms (see § 45, 5, *b*, *c*)? 19. Give an example (or examples), with the meaning, of the following: — Copulative, Disjunctive, Causal, Concessive, and Final. 20. Give some of the most common Interjections, with their meaning.

CONSTRUCTIONS OF SYNTAX.

The preceding Lessons include practice on the forms of Latin inflections, but with such constructions only, as the definitions of the cases, moods, and tenses naturally suggest. Before reading continuous passages, some less obvious constructions must be learned. These are divided into sections of convenient length for single lessons, and may be so studied if the teacher prefer; or he may, at his discretion, proceed at once to reading the annotated passages which follow, taking up each principle as it occurs in practice. In either case, it will aid greatly in the intelligent progress of the learner, if the constructions here given should all be studied and made familiar, before attempting the reading of any author in course. They should be compared, throughout, with the "Synopsis of Constructions" on pp. 248, 249, of the Grammar. In the simpler constructions, the *short rules* § 75 (marked R.) may be substituted at pleasure for the more extended form, when the principle has been made familiar.

A.— Uses of Cases: 1. As Objects of Verbs.

1. The Accusative as Direct Object (§ 52, with 1. *a* and *b*; R. 21).

a. The accusatives in § 52, 1. *a*, are usually rendered with a preposition in English, though sometimes a transitive verb may be supplied: as, **rīdēre**, *to laugh at* or *ridicule;* **dolēre**, *to grieve at* or *lament*, &c.

b. With § 52, 1. *d* compare § 51, 2. *d;* noticing that there is usually no difference in the translation of the two classes of verbs, which are generally transitive in English: as, **adīre aliquem**, *to approach one;* **obstāre alicui**, *to withstand one*.

2. The use of two Accusatives (§ 52, 2 ; R. 25).

3. The Dative as Indirect Object (§ 51, 1, 2, with *a* and *d;* read the classes of verbs in *b;* R. 14, 16).

Several verbs of the list in § 51, 2. *a* (as *to favor, envy, serve*, &c.) seem to be transitive. The fact is, that the Latin retains a primary meaning which is lost in English: as, **invīdēre** (*envy*) is *to look* [askance] *at one;* **servīre** is *to be a slave;* **suādēre** is *to make* [a thing] *pleasant* to any one (compare **suāvis,** *sweet*). See Remark 1, and the second paragraph of the Note on page 121. [The list of verbs in § 51, 2. *a* and *b*, will be learned gradually, in the course of practice.]

4. The Genitive as Object of Memory, Feeling, &c. (§ 50, 4. *a, b, c,* with 1, 2; R. 12).

5. The Ablative with **ūtor,** etc. (§ 56, 6. *d;* R. 31).

NOTE. — The above rules cover the frequent cases in which the Accusative is used after verbs which do not take a direct object in English; also those uses of the Genitive and Dative in which they require to be translated by the English Objective.

B.—Uses of Cases: 2. As Modifying Adjectives.

6. The Genitive following Adjectives (50, 3. *b, c, d*).
Compare the lists of adjectives in § 50, 3. *d*, with that in § 51, 6. *c*. These adjectives, when followed by the genitive, have in fact become nouns (compare § 47, 3): as, **cognātus Cicerōnis,** *Cicero's kinsman;* **Cicerōnī cognātus,** *kindred with Cicero.* [Compare such phrases as **meus aequālis,** *my contemporary.*]

7. The Dative of Nearness, &c. (§ 51, 6; R. 15).

8. The Ablative of *want* (§ 54, 1. *c, d;* R. 28); 9. of *source* (id. 2. *a;* R. 29); 10. of *comparison* (id. 5; R. 32); 11. of *means* (id. 6, with *c;* R. 30); 12. of *difference* (id. 6. *e;* R. 33).

a. Notice that § 54, 5 (ablative of comparison) and 6. *c* (ablative of difference), expressing different relations, may be used together with the same adjective: as, **multō dīvitior Crassō,** *much richer than Crassus.*

b. All the words under § 54, 6. *e,* are either participles, like **abundāns, complētus** ; or were originally participles, as **plēnus.** When used *as pure adjectives,* they take the genitive under § 50, 3. *b*.

c. The ablatives under Rule 30 (§ 75) are of various origin, and must be translated according to the English idiom: as, **dignus,** *worthy of;* **praeditus,** *gifted with,* &c. (compare § 54, 3. *a;* 10. *a*).

NOTE. — Some of the above are also to be classed among the adverbial uses of cases; but they are distinguished by being used to *complete the meaning* of the adjective on which they depend.

C.—Uses of Cases: 3. Miscellaneous.

13. Adverbial Accusative (§ **52**, 3, with *a, b, c;* R. 24).

The accusatives under § **52**, 3. *a*, are usually translated as adverbs (see examples).

14. The Accusative in Exclamations (§ **52**, 4. *a*).

15. Dative of *possession* (§ **51**, 3; R. 17); 16. of *service* (id. 5; R. 20); 17. of *reference* (id. 7).

a. The dative (of service) under § **51**, 5, may sometimes be translated as *predicate nominative;* but more commonly with the preposition OF.

b. The Dative (of reference) in § **51**, 7, merely expresses a *more remote relation* than those under 2 (indirect object): compare the first examples under each.

18. Ablative of *separation* (§ **54**, 1; R. 28); 19. of *cause* (id. 3; R. 26); 20. of *means* (id. 6); 21. of *manner* and *quality* (id. 7, with § **50**, 1. *g*); 22. of *price* (id. 8, with *a,* and § **50**, 1. *i;* R. 11); 23. of *specification* (id. 9); 24. *locative* (id. 10 with *a*).

For the translation of the Ablative of separation (§ **54**, 1), generally by OF or FROM, see examples.

25. Predicate Genitive (§ **50**, 1. *c* and *d*, with the Remark; R. 8).

26. Relations of Time and Space (§ **55**, 1, with *b;* 3, with *a, b, c, d, f;* R. 23, 34, 36).

Compare the Note, § **55**, 3 (Relations of Place), with § **42**, 1, and with the Note on page 113.

D.—Use of Moods and Tenses.

27. Independent uses of the Subjunctive (§ **57**, 2, with *a;* 3, 4, 6; compare § **60**, 2. *a, b;* R. 43).

28. Historical Infinitive (§ **57**, 8. *h;* R. 40).

N. B. The present infinitive (§ **58**, 11), when depending on a past tense, is to be translated by a past tense (see first example); sometimes by the *perfect infinitive* (§ **58**, 11. *a*).

29. The Sequence of Tenses (§ **58**, 9, 10, with 1, 2; learning by heart the Rule and Examples, and reading the Remark carefully).

The perfect and pluperfect subjunctive under this rule may express a *relatively future action*, as representing in indirect discourse the future perfect indicative: as, **si discessisset** = *if he shall depart* (*shall have departed*), &c. — B. G. i. 45.

E. — Subordinate Constructions.

30. CONDITIONAL CLAUSES. — Definitions (§ **59**, with 1, reading the Note).

Commit to memory the models on page 167, with their meaning. Read carefully 3. *a, b;* 4. *a, b, c.*

31. Disguised Conditions (§ **60**, 1, with *a*).

32. Conditional Particles (§ **61**, 1, with Remark).

Observe that with these particles the subj. present is translated like the imperfect in §.59, 3. *b* (condition contrary to fact).

33. TEMPORAL CLAUSES. — Absolute and Relative Time (§ **62**, 2, reading the Note).

34. The Particles **ubi, postquam**, etc. (id. 2. *a*).

35. The construction of **cum** *temporal* (id. 2. *b*).

36. **Cum** *causal* or *concessive* (id. *e*).

a. **Cum** followed by the present or perfect subjunctive is almost always CAUSAL, and is to be translated *since, while,* or *although*.

b. **Cum** followed by the imperfect or pluperfect subjunctive is more commonly TEMPORAL. In this case, it is sometimes to be translated *when;* but is often best rendered by a *participle, present* or *perfect,* in English.

37. PURPOSE: with **ut, quo, ne** (§ **64**, 1).

This is often to be translated *may* or *might;* but oftener *by the simple infinitive*.

38. RESULT: clause of Characteristic (§ **65**, 2).

This is to be translated variously according to the context (see examples under *a, b, c, d, e, f,* noticing particularly *e*).

N. B. The above are the only cases in which the Subjunctive affects the translation into English.

39. DEPENDENT: relative or conditional (R. 47; read § **66**, with 1 and 2; compare § **67**, 1).

F.—Substantive Clauses.

40. Classification (§ **70**, 1; reading the Definition and Remark).

41. Accusative and Infinitive (§ **70**, 2; comparing § 67 and 1, *indirect discourse;* also § 57, 8. *e;* R. 39).

The English word of indirect discourse is THAT; but it is frequently well to omit the *that* in translation, or even to change to direct discourse as if the clause were independent. These clauses come after any word of *seeing, saying, thinking,* and the like.

42. Substantive clauses of *purpose* (§ **70**, 3).

These may be translated by THAT with the auxiliaries *may, might, shall, should;* but often by the simple Infinitive.

43. Substantive clauses of *result* (§ **70**, 4).

These may be translated by THAT, with or without the auxiliaries *can, could;* occasionally by the simple Infinitive; sometimes by the participial noun in -ING (see examples under *g*), especially after verbs of hindering.

In general, the learner may be advised to use the Infinitive in rendering a Latin object-clause, *wherever the English idiom permits.*

44. The Clause with **quod** (§ **70**, 5).

This is generally to be translated by THAT, or THE FACT THAT; occasionally by WHEREAS.

45. Indirect Questions (§ **67**, 2, and read the Remark; R. 45).

Observe that an Indirect Question occurs only when an *interrogative clause* (or one introduced by an interrogative word) *is made the subject or object of some verb*, or equivalent phrase. Thus the words *who is there?* are a DIRECT QUESTION; in the sentence *I do not know* [it is uncertain] *who is there*, the same words are an INDIRECT QUESTION. This form is to be carefully distinguished from dependent RELATIVE clauses under 39, above; also from direct questions in the subjunctive mood (*dubitative subjunctive*): as, **quid faciam,** *what shall I do?* **quid facerem?** *what was I to do?*

G.—Participial Constructions.

46. Predicate use of Participles (§ **72**, 1, with *b*; 2, 3, 4).

In these constructions, the translation must be varied to conform to the English idiom (see § 72, 3, with the Remark).

47. Ablative Absolute (§ **54**, 10. *b*, reading the Note; R. 35).

a. The Ablative Absolute is very rarely found except with the *present active* and the *perfect passive* participle. It is generally to be rendered, when possible, by an active construction in English.

b. As the Nominative Absolute is rarely admissible in English, a change of form is generally required in translation. Thus the present participle is oftenest to be rendered by a relative clause with *when* or *while;* and the perfect passive participle by the perfect active participle in English. These changes may be seen in the following example:—

"At illi, *intermisso spatio, imprudentibus nostris*, atque *occupatis* in munitione castrorum, subito se ex silvis ejecerunt; *impetu*que in eos *facto*, qui erant in statione pro castris collocati, acriter pugnaverunt; *duabusque missis* subsidio cohortibus a Caesare, cum hae (*perexiguo intermisso* loci *spatio* inter se) constitissent, novo genere pugnae *perterritis nostris*, per medios audacissime perruperunt, seque inde incolumes receperunt."—CÆSAR, B. G. v. 15.

"But they, *having paused a space while our men* were *unaware* and *busied* in fortifying the camp, suddenly threw themselves out of the woods; then *making an attack* upon those who were on guard in front of the camp, fought fiercely; and, *though two cohorts had been sent* to their relief by Cæsar, after these had taken their position (*leaving very little space* of ground between them), *as our men were alarmed* by the strange kind of fighting, they dashed most daringly through the midst of them, and got off safe."

48. Gerundive Constructions (§ **72**, 5. *c*; § **73**, 2; R. 41).

NOTE.—In this Gerundive use the form in **dus** is always ACTIVE (translated by a participial noun followed by the objective); in the Predicate use it is always PASSIVE (translated *ought, must, &c.;* see Lesson 21, 2, *f*).

DERIVATION OF WORDS.

THE Derivation of Words is one of the most important branches of Grammar. No one can know a language by study unless he becomes able to analyze its words and group them together, as "families," in their natural classification. Especially no progress can be made in *reading at sight* — practically the most valuable thing in the knowledge of a language — without a good acquaintance with its formative part.

The exercises here given are intended to aid in acquiring this knowledge; and they are followed by a selection of passages, in reading which it is expected that the learner will be guided not merely by the *dictionary meaning* of the words, but (so far as may be) by the meanings of root or stem, and terminations, as explained by the laws of derivation and the groupings of *families* of words. As introductory to these, he should learn § **44** (general definition), with 1 and *a;* and read *b* carefully, with the Note. The teacher should illustrate the exercises throughout on the blackboard, so as to inculcate the true idea of language as *built up from Roots by means of originally significant terminations* (" Stem-building ").

NOTE. — It is not expected that the pupil should fully understand the illustrations under *b;* but only that he should learn to distinguish readily between the root and its derivatives. Even when the meaning of the root cannot be exactly determined, but is found in a group or family of words, — or when the formative part is uncertain in the same way, — the habit thus acquired is a very great aid in mastering the Vocabulary.

1. Learn carefully the meaning of the following *significant endings* (§ **44**, 1. *c*), and show their force in the accompanying derivatives: —

   1. **tor, trix** : — *arator* (aro, *plough*); *cultrix* (colo, *cultivate*).

Notice that the t becomes s in the same verbs that have the supine in s (see § 30, 3. *f;* 1. 3 *f*⁴).

   2. **io, tio** : *opinio* (opīnor, *think*); *sessio* (sĕdeo, *sit*).

Derivation of Words. 53

3. men, mentum: *flumen* (fluo, *flow*); *frumentum* (fruor, *enjoy*).
4. ulus, olus, ellus, culus: *rivulus* (rīvus, *stream*); *gladiolus* (gladius, *sword*); *puella* (puer, *boy*); *munusculum* (mūnus, *gift*).
5. itās, itūdo, ia (of which the i belongs to the stem of the primitive): *caritas* (cārus, *dear*); *magnitudo* (magnus, *great*); *absentia* (absens, *absent*).
6. ānus, ensis: *Romanus* (Rōma, *Rome*); *Siciliensis* (Sicilia, *Sicily*).
7. ides, ades, is; *Priamides* (Priamus, *Priam*); *Tyndaris* (Tyndarus); *Atlantiades* (Atlas).
8. ālis, āris, ilis: *tribunalis* (tribūnus, *tribune*); *militaris* (mīles, *soldier*); *hostilis* (hostis, *enemy*).
9. eus, āceus: *aureus* (aurum, *gold*); *cretaceus* (crēta, *chalk*).
10. ōsus, tus: *copiosus* (cōpia, *plenty*); *auritus* (auris, *ear*).
11. āx, idus, bundus: *pugnax* (pugno, *fight*); *lucidus* (lūceo, *shine*); *moribundus* (morior, *die*).
12. ilis, bilis (passive verbal): *fragilis* (frango); *nobilis* (nosco).

2. Use the list given on pages 97, 98, in determining the meaning of the following words, with the force of the significant ending (consulting the lexicon when necessary); bearing in mind that derivatives are formed from *roots* and *stems*, not from nominatives or present tenses, etc.

1. victor; 2. cēnsor; 3. genetrīx; 4. mēnsūra; 5. dēmentia; 6. legio; 7. hospitium; 8. cognōmen; 9. amplitūdo; 10. levitās; 11. innocentia; 12. spectāculum; 13. fīliolus; 14. Atrīdes; 15. Nereīs; 16. Crētēnsis; 17. Fidēnās; 18. vitulīna (caro); 19. ovīle; 20. arbustum; 21. paluster; 22. patrīcius; 23. aerumnōsus; 24. edāx; 25. timidus; 26. egregius; 27. recidīvus; 28. habilis; 29. acidulus; 30. dīversōrium; 31. alumnus; 32. argentārius; 33. spectābilis; 34. timor; 35. majusculus; 36. facilis; 37. rapidus; 38. trepidus; 39. tremulus; 40. diuturnus; 41. apiārium.

As an example of analysis for the purpose of determining meaning, take the word **pābulātio**. The termination **tio** is seen to be a "verbal abstract;" that is, to express, in a general or abstract way, the action of a verb. The long **ā** points to a verb of the first conjugation (2. a^1), formed from an adjective or noun of the first or second declension. This leads us to the noun **pābulum**; and the verb would signify *doing something* with that noun. In c^2 (last line), **bulum** is found as a termination of nouns of *means :* **pābulum** is the means of doing the action expressed in the root PA. As roots are not given in our lexicons, we must learn to recognize them in the *present stems* of verbs (see Lesson 28). If the pupil now finds or has already learned the meaning of **pascor**, he can see that **pābulum** is a means of *feeding;* **pābulor** (deponent) is *to obtain* (say) *the means of feeding;* and **pābulātio** (in the connection where we find it) can only mean *foraging.*

Other examples might be found, as in **dōnatīvus** (from **dōnum**, root DA, termination **aa**), through **dōno** and part. **dōnātus**; **peregrīnātio** (from per-ager ; root AG, termination ra); and so on, to any extent. The teacher will do well to encourage the practice of analyzing words on the above model, but not of course to carry it so far as to weary the pupil.

Even when the meaning of the root does not appear at all, the grouping of the derivations may still be very instructive. Thus, **humus**, *ground;* **humilis**, *low* (on the ground); **homo** (-in; see I, *b*, N.), *man* (creature of earth); **hūmānus**, *gentle* (as belonging to man in distinction from brutes); **hūmānitās**, *gentleness* or *refinement.* When the learner comes to the Greek χαμαί, *on the ground*, he will recognize it as of the same derivation ; and his curiosity may be gratified by learning that the same root is found in the German *Bräutigam* and the English *bridegroom.*

The chief advantage, however, is in the knowledge of immediate and conscious derivatives. Thus, **aedīlicius** can only mean *belonging to an ædile*, while **aedīlis** itself must have something to do with public *edifices* (aedi-ficia); **sermunculus** must mean *a little talk;* **esurio**, *desire to eat*, hence *to be hungry;* **emāx**, *eager to buy*, and so on. Compare, for illustration, the following words from one root : **medeor, medicus medicīna, medicīnālis, medicor, medicāmentum, medicāmentārius, medicābilis, medicamentōsus, meditor** (frequentative, with an earlier meaning preserved). Notice the modes of formation in the foregoing words.

3. Explain the meaning and force of the termination in each of the following derivative verbs, giving the form of the primitive : —

1. flōresco; 2. capesso; 3. dictito; 4. jacto; 5. cantillo; 6. empturio; 7. timesco; 8. cēsso; 9. agito; 10. calesco; 11. laudo; 12. mīlito; 13. insānio; 14. flōreo; 15. salveo; 16. sector; 17. dominor; 18. sitio.

Derivation of Words. 55

4. Explain the meaning and derivation of the following compounds, using the vocabulary when necessary (§ 44, 3): —

1. mātricīda; 2. suŏvetaurīlia; 3. longimanus; 4. signifer; 5. āliger; 6. artifex; 7. cornicen; 8. princeps; 9. praeceps; 10. discors; 11. pusillanimus; 12. quintuplex; 13. benefacio; 14. adfero (affero); 15. aufero (abfero); 16. obfero (offero); 17. ambitus; 18. reditus; 19. redditus; 20. sēcerno; 21. portendo; 22. amputo; 23. computo; 24. crēdo; 25. nāvigo; 26. biennium; 27. sēmestris.

The analysis of the above words will either suggest the meaning, or at any rate fix it in the memory. Thus, suovetaurīlia can only mean something to do with a *swine*, a *sheep*, and a *bull;* and, if we learn the habit of the Romans to put the names of sacrifices and feasts in the neuter plural, we shall know the word at its first appearance.

Even if no advantage were gained in acquiring or retaining the meaning, yet the words become more interesting and lively, and the knowledge of them more intelligent and fruitful. Thus in **redintegrātio** we have the prefix **red-**, *back again* (to its former state); the ending **-tio** (verbal abstract); the verb is **integro (āre)**, denominative from **integer**, *whole* or *sound* (**in**, *not;* TAG, root of **tango**, *touch;* **ra**, participial = *tus* or *nus*): hence the meaning *restoration* (making uninjured again).

In such derivatives as **amputo, computo**, the meanings seem absurdly inconsistent. But the verb is a *denominative* from the adjective **putus**, a collateral form of **purus**, *clean* (see 1, *b*). The corresponding verb (which would be **puo**) is lost; but its original sense appears in **puto**, *to clean up* (as by trimming off a diseased branch), and also *to clear up* (as an account), and so *to reckon*, then *to think*, which meanings are divided between the above compounds.

5. Form words with the following meanings from the accompanying primitives: —

1. *A reckoning* (**reor**, *reckon*); 2. *An assembly* (**convenio**, *come together*); 3. *Arrangement* (**dispōno**, *distribute*); 4. *A change* (**verto**. *turn*); 5. *A joining* (**jungo**); 6. *A breaking* (**frango**); 7. *Length* (**longus**); 8. *Breadth* (**lātus**); 9. *Power of holding* (**capāx** from **capio**, *take*); 10. *Means of teaching* (**doceo**); 11. *Means of support* (**colo**); 12. *Means of covering* (**tego**); 13. *Brightness* (**clārus**); 14. *Softness* (**mollis**, *soft*); 15. *Sweetness*

(suāvis); 16. *Means of trying* (ex-perior); 17. *A tray* (for carrying: fero); 18. *A piece broken* (frango); 19. *Means of feeding* (alo); 20. *A bramble-thicket* (dumus); 21. *A rose-garden* (rosa); 22. *A dove-cote* (columba); 23. *Lamentable* (fleo); 24. *Made of flowers* (flōs); 25. *Blooming* (flōreo); 26. *Sickly* (morbus); 27. *Commerce* (mercor); 28. *A mingling* (misceo); 29. *Belonging to a soldier* (mīles); 30. *To grow mild* (mītis); 31. *A little measure* (modus); 32. *A little pattern* (forma); 33. *A little man* (homo); 34. *A little puppy* (catulus); 35. *A means of defence* (mūnio); 36. *Changeable* (mūto); 37. *Teachable* (doceo); 38. *With a large nose* (nasus); 39. *With horns* (cornū); 40. *Bearded* (barba); 41. *Belonging to a ship* (nāvis); 42. *Sinewy* (nervus); 43. *Snowy* (nix); 44. *A little eye* (oculus): 45. *Son of Priam* (Priamus).

READING AT SIGHT.

Constant practice in reading at sight is the surest way to secure a practical acquaintance with the vocabulary and grammar of any language. Much time and labor are wasted in learning merely *about the languages* we study, instead of studying *the languages themselves*, or the ideas expressed in them. It is one thing to be able to read passages which we have already studied; but quite a different thing to have such knowledge of a language, that its words at once suggest corresponding ideas, and its moods, tenses, cases, &c., suggest their right logical relations.

Few learners are aware how much the latter kind of knowledge — how much even of the power and skill (or knack) of getting it — may be acquired by practice. To aid in its acquisition, the learner is desired to bear in mind the following directions: —

1. Look first at *the endings of words*, so as to become instantly aware of their grammatical relations.

This it is not natural for an English-speaking person to do. The habit of it must be formed by practice; and the earlier the practice is formed, the better.

2. Observe the *significant endings* (§ 44, 1. *c*), and always connect obvious derivatives with their primitives.

3. Even where derivations are not obvious, *group words in families*, so as to associate their meanings.

In many cases, the succession of words in the lexicon will be sufficient to suggest these groups. Notice what in the words is like and what is unlike; what words mean with a given root or stem, and what effect is given by a different termination.

4. Associate the Latin words with *English derivatives*, however remote; and with other languages if you happen to know any.

5. Use any mechanical device or "thumb-rule" possible, as to the *position of words*, or their probable meanings in such and such connections.

6. Commit to memory phrases, or (if possible) whole passages.

To cultivate the memory merely in the way of learning the rules and principles of grammar is one great obstacle to the right knowledge of a language. A passage of Cicero, a dozen verses of Virgil, or an Ode of Horace, thoroughly studied and learned by heart, would, with far less outlay of labor, teach far more of the language than an equal bulk of grammatical rules.

7. Notice constantly such idioms, or modes of expression, as are like or unlike our own.

8. In translating aloud, always use the English idiom; but *take in the Latin first in its own idiom;* if possible, without even thinking of the corresponding English words.

The form of expression, or the order of words, that seems most natural to us, is very rarely that which would occur to a Roman mind, or be found in a Latin sentence. The art of good translation consists first in adjusting ourselves readily to a foreign mode of thought or speech, and then reproducing it, independently, in the form natural to our own tongue.

9. In translating any word, always bear in mind its *leading or principal meaning*.

This is not always the etymological meaning, though it may be usually traced to that; but it is the *conscious meaning* (as it were), the notion which the Roman himself attached to it. For example, the leading meaning of **mitto** seems to be, *let go*, either with or without accompanying effort; and this meaning the Roman felt in it, though we may translate it by different expressions. Thus, **mittere tēlum**, *to throw a weapon;* **mittere legātōs**, *to send ambassadors;* **mittere aliquam rem** (often), *to let a thing go, to omit or pass over a thing;* hence, **mittere lacrimas**, *to cease weeping;* **mittere dicere**, *to forbear saying* (see **mitto** in Lexicon).

You should never select a meaning in the dictionary, without seeing (as in this case) what the original meaning is, which we may be sure was present to the mind of a Roman. When we learn a language *from the inside out*, — as we do our own, — we do this by an unconscious generalization from a great number of usages. This is of course the best way to learn a language, if we have time; but in order to learn a language *from the outside in*, — as we do in the case of Latin, — we must do the same thing by conscious study.

We may even say that this is more necessary in using a good dictionary than in using a poor one; for a good one gives meanings which — being correct in the corresponding English phrase — give a very inaccurate reflection of the true meaning of the word. Thus, **capere poenās** means in English *to inflict punishment;* but to a Roman it meant to *receive* or *exact the penalty* for a wrong. So also with the relations of words. Cæsar says that Orgetorix was required to plead his cause **ex vinculis**, for which our translation must be *in chains;* though this is exactly the opposite of what Cæsar says, viz. that, standing in chains, he should make his plea *from them*.

A few short passages are here appended, in order to illustrate the foregoing points, and show how to go to work.

1. Matrem*ᵃ* Phalaridis*ᵇ* scribit*ᶜ* Ponticus Heraclides, doctus*ᵈ* vir, auditor et discipulus Platonis, visam esse*ᵉ* videre in somnis*ᶠ* simulacra*ᵍ* deorum, quae*ʰ* ipsa domi consecravisset;*ⁱ* ex iis*ᵏ* Mercurium*ˡ* e patera,*ᵐ* quam dextera manu teneret, sanguinem visum esse fundere,*ⁿ* qui cum terram attigisset,*ᵒ* refervescere*ᵖ* videretur, sic ut tota domus sanguine redundaret.*ᑫ* Quod matris somnium*ʳ* immanis*ˢ* filii crudelitas comprobavit. — *De Divinatione*, i. 23.

a. Notice that the first word is an accusative, **mātrem**. This must probably be either the object of a verb, or the subject of an infinitive: it can remain in suspense till the verb appears. Its meaning, *mother*, naturally suggests a genitive: This we find in

b. **Phalaridis**, which has the genitive ending of the third declension; its nominative must be *Phalaris*, obviously a proper name. We may learn elsewhere that it is that of a Sicilian tyrant.

c. The verb **scrībit**, *writes*, from its meaning naturally suggests an object-clause, accusative with infinitive. Such clauses are often best rendered by direct discourse in English. Thus we may translate as if **mātrem** were nominative: *the mother of Phalaris, writes Pontius Heraclides* (obviously a proper name, and subject of **scrībit**).

d. The next words, being nominative, are probably in apposition with the name: **doctus** (participle of **doceo**) is *taught*, but as an adjective must be *learned*; **audītor** (noun of agency from **audio**) is *hearer*; **discipulus** (connected with **disco**) is clearly the same as our *disciple*; **Platōnis** (as *Phalaridis*, above) explains itself.

e. As we have been expecting an infinitive for an object-clause, **vīsam esse** (having its participle in the feminine) is the natural verb for **mātrem**; and as we have learned that the passive of **video** means *seem*, we may translate (in direct discourse, as above) with **vidēre**, *seemed to see*.

f. In the phrase **in somnīs**, the noun is probably ablative, since the connection requires *in* rather than *into*; and comes from **somnus**, or -**ā**, or -**um**. Some English derivative will probably suggest the meaning *sleep*; and the plural form, though odd, will give no trouble.

g. The next is a new word, but may be analyzed. The termination -**orum**, denoting *means*, is appended to a verb-stem **simula-**: hence the verb is **simulo, āre**, suggesting the English verb *simulate* or perhaps the adjective *similar*. Its meaning will be *something to represent*; and we may render the phrase **simulācra deōrum**, *images of the gods*.

h. The relative **quae** naturally refers to a noun just preceding: this cannot be **deōrum**, which is masculine, and must be **simulācra**; **ipsa** might agree with **quae**, but will be more easily taken with the verb next following.

i. This verb, **consecrāvisset**, at once suggests the English *consecrate*. It is evidently a compound with **con**; and if we remember the common change of vowel in compound verbs, and connect its meaning with **sacer**, *sacred* (already given), this meaning will be confirmed. The subjunctive form (see above, 37) does not affect the translation, which is by the simple indicative, because our idiom does not require any other mood.

k. The ablative **iis** will refer to the last or most important *plural noun*, either **deōrum** or **simulācra**, it will not matter which. The phrase may be rendered *one of these*.

l. **Mercurium** may be assumed to continue the same construction as **mātrem**, and will take the infinitive **vīsum esse**, below.

m. **Patera** may be left as not important for the meaning of the whole: we may, for the present, call it "*something*" *which he held in his right hand* (the relative clause here explaining itself): in fact, *a shallow bowl*.

n. The infinitive **fundere** must be guessed at from the context or given by the teacher, unless its meaning is known, *to pour*.

o. The verb **attigisset**, as a glance shows, contains the root TAG found in **tango**, *touch;* the subjunctive is required by **cum**, and does not affect the translation; its subject is **qui**, referring to the masculine **sanguinem**. But as two relatives cannot come together in English, we translate, *and when this had touched the ground.*

p. The verb **refervescere** should be seen to be derivative, and compounded from **ferveo**, which associates it with *fervent, fervid;* and its meaning, *to boil up*, is seen from our word *effervescent...*

q. The meaning of **redundāret** (*overflowed*) may perhaps require to be given, though a tolerably close idea may be gained by conjecture. Following **ut**, it is subjunctive expressing a result.

r. The phrase **quod somnium** may be either nominative or accusative; but, as the verb is directly preceded by the nominative **crūdelitās**, these words must be accusative, and the object of **comprobāvit**. The meaning of **somnium** (*dream*), if not known, may be easily inferred from **somnus**, above.

s. The adjective **immānis** may be either genitive with **fīlii** or nominative with **crūdelitās**: consider which needs an epithet. Its meaning (*monstrous*) will require to be given, as also that of **comprobāvit** (*proved*), which should, however, be explained through the adjective **probus**, and kindred English words.

The above analysis is given in much greater detail than will often be required in practice. When the habit has once been formed, it is followed rapidly and almost unconsciously; in fact, it is impossible, when once the mind has been trained to it, to read a single sentence without deriving help from it. In succeeding passages, only a few hints will be given.

2. Hoc item in Sileni *Graeca historia* est: Hannibalem, cum cepisset Saguntum, visum esse in somnis a Jove in deorum concilium vocari; quo cum venisset, Jovem imperavisse ut Italiae bellum inferret; ducemque ei unum e concilio datum, quo illum utentem cum exercitu progredi coepisse. Tum ei ducem illum praecepisse ne respiceret; illum autem id diutius facere non potuisse, elatumque cupiditate respexisse. Tum visam beluam vastam et immanem, circumplicatam serpentibus, quacumque incederet omnia arbusta, virgulta, tesca pervertere; et eum admiratum quaesisse de deo, quodnam illud esset tale monstrum. Et deum respondisse *Vastitatem esse Italiae*, praecepisseque ut pergeret protinus: quid retro atque a tergo fieret ne laboraret. — *id.* i. 24.

This passage may be somewhat harder than the foregoing, but a little attention will show that it is in the same general construction, — "*Hannibalem . . . visum esse*" like "*matrem . . . visam esse*," — and that it contains several of the words and phrases already explained. It will greatly simplify the rendering of a passage like this, to drop the form of indirect discourse, beginning with the leading subject: *Hannibal, having taken Saguntum, seemed in his sleep to be summoned, &c.*: all the infinitives being translated by indicatives, and the subjunctive **laboraret** as an infinitive, *not to trouble himself*. A number of words must of course be suggested.

3. L. Paulus, consul iterum, cum ei bellum [a] ut cum rege Perse gereret obtigisset, ut [b] ea ipsa die domum ad vesperum rediit, [b] filiolam [c] suam Tertiam, quae tum erat admodum parva, osculans animum advertit [c] tristiculam. 'Quid est,' inquit, 'mea Tertia? quid tristis es?' 'Mi pater,' inquit, 'Persa periit.' Tum ille artius puellam complexus, 'Accipio,' inquit, 'mea filia, omen.' Erat autem mortuus catellus eo nomine. — *id.* i. 46.

a. In this passage, — as we find it hard, with our habit of speech, to carry so many words in the mind undisposed of, — it may be necessary after **bellum** to look for the verb to which it belongs. As **ut** is a relative word, the nearest verb will belong to that; so that we must take the next following, **obtigisset**, the meaning of which must be given (in connection with the root TAG); the object of **gereret** must be supplied from **bellum**; and it will read, *when the war had fallen to his lot to wage with king Perses*. This is not a good translation; but, having seen the Latin idea in this way, you can easily find a corresponding English expression: *It had fallen, &c.*

b. To translate **ut**, notice at once *the mood of its verb;* because the two uses of **ut** have meanings very far apart in English, though the Romans did not probably feel the difference. As the verb is here indicative, **ut** means *as* or *when:* **rediit** (red, *back;* eo, *go*) signifies *returned*.

c. The word **filiolam**, diminutive of **filia**, explains itself; while **animum advertit**, *turned his mind*, is to be rendered as a single transitive verb, *observed;* and its subject is **L. Paulus**.

4. Scipio Nasica cum ad poetam Ennium venisset, eique ab ostio quaerenti*ᵃ* Ennium ancilla dixisset domi non esse;*ᵇ* Nasica sensit, illam domini jussu dixisse et illum intus esse. Paucis post diebus, cum ad Nasicam venisset Ennius, et cum a janua quaereret, exclamat Nasica, se domi non esse. Tum Ennius, 'Quid,' inquit, 'ego non cognosco vocem tuam?' Hic Nasica, "Homo es impudens; ego cum quaererem, ancillae tuae credidi, te*ᶜ* domi non esse; tu mihi non credis ipsi.'

a. To him inquiring, &c. can only mean *when he inquired for Ennius*.

b. The subject of the infinitive is here wanting, a rare usage in Latin; but it is obviously *Ennius*, to be supplied from the preceding.

c. The clause **te domi non esse** is evidently a secondary object of **credidi**; but, as *believe* does not take two objects in English, some word like *saying* must be supplied.

SELECTIONS.

[The figures refer to the Constructions of Syntax, pages 46–51.]

1. *A Haunted House.*

1. Erat Athenis [26] spatiosa et capax domus; sed infamis et pestilens: per silentium noctis sonus ferri, et, si attenderes [30] acrius, strepitus vinculorum, longius primo, deinde e proximo, reddebatur: mox apparebat idolon, senex macie [20] et squalore confectus, promissa barba,[21] horrenti capillo: cruribus compedes manibus catenas gerebat, quatiebatque.

2. Inde inhabitantibus tristes diraeque noctes per metum vigilabantur: vigiliam morbus, et, crescente formidine, mors sequebatur. Nam interdiu quoque, quamquam abscesserat imago, memoria imaginis oculis inerrabat; longiorque causis [10] timor erat. Deserta inde et damnata solitudine domus, totaque illi monstro relicta; proscribebatur tamen, seu quis emere, seu quis conducere, ignarus tanti mali, vellet.[29]

3. Venit Athenas [26] philosophus Athenodorus: legit titulum; auditoque pretio,[47] quia suspecta vilitas, percontatus,[46] omnia [2] docetur, ac nihilo [11] minus, immo tanto magis, conducit. Ubi coepit advesperascere, jubet sterni (sc. *lectum*) sibi prima domus parte: poscit pugillares, stilum, lumen: suos omnes in interiora dimittit; ipse ad scribendum animum, oculos, manum intendit, ne vacua mens audita simulacra et inanes sibi [17] metus fingeret.[37]

4. Initio,[26] quale ubique, silentium noctis: deinde concuti [28] ferrum, vincula moveri. Ille non tollere [28]

oculos, non remittere stilum, sed obfirmare animum, auribusque praetendere. Tum crebrescere fragor, adventare, et jam ut in limine, jam ut intra limen, audiri. Respicit: videt agnoscitque narratam sibi effigiem. Stabat, innuebatque digito, similis vocanti.⁷ Hic, contra, ut paulum ²⁶ exspectaret ⁴² manu significat; rursusque ceris ³ et stilo incumbit.

5. Illa scribentis capiti catenis insonabat. Respicit rursus, idem quod prius ¹³ innuentem: nec moratus, tollit lumen, et sequitur. Ibat illa lento gradu, quasi gravis vinculis.¹¹ Postquam deflexit ³⁴ in aream domus, repente dilapsa deserit comitem; desertus herbas et folia concerpta signum loco ponit.

6. Postero die ²⁶ adit magistratus;¹ monet, ut illum locum effodi jubeant.⁴² Inveniuntur ossa inserta catenis et implicita, quae corpus aevo ¹⁹ terraque putrefactum nuda et exesa reliquerat vinculis: ²⁶ collecta ⁴⁶ publice sepeliuntur: domus postea, rite conditis manibus, caruit.
—*Pliny, Epist.* vii. 27.

II. *A Sharper of Syracuse.*

1. C. Canius, eques Romanus, nec infacetus, et satis literatus, cum se Syracusas, otiandi (ut ipse dicere solebat) non negotiandi causa,¹⁹ contulisset,³⁵ dictitabat, se hortulos aliquos velle emere,⁴¹ quo invitare amicos, et ubi se oblectare sine interpellatoribus posset.³⁷ Quod cum percrebuisset,³⁵ Pythius ei quidam, qui argentariam faceret ³⁸ Syracusis, dixit, venales quidem se hortos non habere, sed licere (sc. *cis*) uti Canio,³ si vellet,³⁹ ut suis: ⁵ et simul ad cenam hominem in hortos invitavit in posterum diem.

2. Cum ille promisisset, tum Pythius (qui esset,³⁹ ut argentarius, apud omnes ordines gratiosus) piscatores

ad se convocavit, et ab his petivit, ut ante suos hortulos postridie piscarentur:[42] dixitque, quid eos facere vellet.[45] Ad cenam tempore venit Canius: opipare a Pythio apparatum convivium: cymbarum ante oculos multitudo: pro se quisque, quod ceperat, adferebat: ante pedes Pythi pisces abiciebantur.

3. Tum Canius, 'Quaeso,' inquit, 'quid est hoc, Pythi? tantumne piscium, tantumne cymbarum?' Et ille, 'Quid mirum?' inquit. 'Hoc loco est, Syracusis quidquid est piscium: haec aquatio: hac villa[8] isti carere non possunt.' Incensus Canius cupiditate, contendit a Pythio, ut venderet. Gravate ille primo. Quid multa? impetrat: emit homo cupidus et locuples, tanti,[22] quanti Pythius voluit; et emit instructos: nomina facit: negotium conficit.

4. Invitat Canius postridie familiares suos. Venit ipse mature. Scalmum nullum videt. Quaerit ex proximo vicino, num feriae quaedam piscatorum essent,[45] quod eos nullos videret.[39] 'Nullae, quod sciam,' inquit ille: 'sed hic piscari nulli solent: itaque heri mirabar, quid accidisset.'

5. Stomachari[28] Canius, sed quid faceret?[27] nondum enim Aquillius, collega et familiaris meus, protulerat de dolo malo formulas: in quibus ipsis cum ex eo quaereretur, *Quid esset dolus malus;* respondebat, *Cum esset aliud simulatum, aliud actum.* — Cicero, De Off. iii. 14.

III. *The Vale of Enna.*

1. Vetus est haec opinio, judices, quae constat ex antiquissimis Graecorum litteris ac monumentis, insulam Siciliam[41] totam esse[40] Cereri[3] et Liberae consecratam. Hoc cum ceterae gentes sic arbitrantur, tum ipsi

Siculis ita persuasum est, ut in animis eorum insitum atque innatum esse videatur.[88] Nam et natas esse has in iis locis deas et fruges in ea terra primum repertas esse arbitrantur et raptam esse Liberam, quam eamdem Proserpinam vocant, ex Hennensium nemore: qui locus, quod in media est insula situs, umbilicus Siciliae nominatur. Quam cum investigare et conquirere Ceres vellet,[35] dicitur inflammasse taedas iis ignibus,[20] qui ex Aetnae vertice erumpunt: quas sibi[3] cum ipsa praeferret, orbem omnem peragrasse terrarum.

2. Henna autem, ubi ea quae dico gesta esse memorantur, est loco[24] perexcelso atque edito, quo in summo est aequata agri planities et aquae peremnes, tota vero omni aditu circumcisa atque directa est: quam circa lacus lucique sunt plurimi atque laetissimi flores omni tempore[26] anni, locus ut ipse raptum illum virginis, quem jam a pueris accepimus, declarare videatur.[38]

3. Etenim prope est spelunca quaedam, conversa ad aquilonem, infinita altitudine,[2] qua Ditem patrem ferunt repente cum curru exstitisse abreptamque ex eo loco virginem secum asportasse, et subito non longe a Syracusis penetrasse sub terras, lacumque in eo loco repente exstitisse: ubi usque ad hoc tempus Syracusani festos dies anniversarios agunt celeberrimo virorum mulierumque conventu.[20]

4. Propter hujus opinionis vetustatem, quod horum in iis locis vestigia ac prope incunabula reperiuntur deorum, mira quaedam tota Sicilia[26] privatim ac publice religio est Cereris Hennensis. Etenim multa saepe prodigia vim ejus numenque declarant: multis saepe in difficillimis rebus praesens auxilium ejus oblatum est, ut haec insula ab ea non solum diligi, sed etiam incoli custodirique videatur.[29] — *id. in Verr.* v. 48.

IV. *The Earth is made for Man.*

1. Terra vero feta frugibus et vario leguminum genere, quae cum maxima largitate fundit, ea ferarumne an hominum causa gignere videtur? Quid de vitibus olivetisque dicam? quarum uberrimi laetissimique fructus nihil omnino ad bestias pertinent. Neque enim serendi neque colendi nec tempestive demetendi percipiendique fructus, neque condendi ac reponendi ulla pecudum scientia est, earumque omnium rerum hominum [25] est et usus et cura.

2. Ut fides igitur et tibias eorum causa factas dicendum est, qui illis uti possent, sic ea, quae diximus, iis solis confitendum est esse parata, qui utuntur; nec si quae bestiae furantur aliquid ex iis aut rapiunt, illarum quoque causa ea nata esse dicemus. Neque enim homines murum aut formicarum causa frumentum condunt, sed conjugum et liberorum et familiarum suarum. Itaque bestiae furtim (ut dixi) fruuntur, domini palam et libere.

3. Tantumque abest ut haec bestiarum etiam causa parata sint,[43] ut ipsas bestias hominum gratia generatas esse videamus.[36] Quid enim oves aliud adferunt, nisi ut earum villis confectis atque contextis homines vestiantur? Quae quidem neque ali neque sustentari neque ullum fructum edere ex se sine cultu hominum et curatione potuissent.[31]

4. Canum vero tam fida custodia tamque amans dominorum adulatio tantumque odium in externos et tam incredibilis ad investigandum sagacitas narium, tanta alacritas in venando quid significat aliud nisi se ad hominum commoditates esse generatos?

5. Quid de bobus loquar? quorum ipsa terga declarant non esse se ad onus accipiendum [48] figurata, cervices autem natae ad jugum, tum vires humerorum et

latitudines ad aratra extrahenda. Quibus, cum terrae subigerentur fissione glaebarum, ab illo aureo genere (ut poëtae loquuntur) vis nulla umquam adferebatur.

Ferrea tum vero proles exorta repente est,
Ausaque funestum prima est fabricarier ensem,
Et gustare manu vinctum domitumque juvencum.

Tanta putabatur utilitas percipi ex bobus, ut eorum visceribus vesci scelus haberetur.

6. Longum est mulorum persequi utilitates et asinorum, quae certe ad hominum usum paratae sunt. Sus vero quid habet praeter escam? Cui quidem, ne putesceret, animam ipsam pro sale datam dicit esse Chrysippus. Qua pecude,[10] quod[13] erat ad vescendum hominibus apta,[7] nihil genuit natura fecundius.

7. Quid multitudinem suavitatemque piscium dicam, quid avium? ex quibus tanta percipitur voluptas, ut interdum Pronoea nostra Epicurea fuisse videatur. Atque hae ne caperentur[37] quidem, nisi hominum ratione atque sollertia, quamquam aves quasdam et alites et oscines, ut nostri augures appellant, rerum[46] augurandarum causa esse natas putamus.

8. Jam vero immanes et feras beluas nanciscimur venando, ut et vescamur iis[5] et exerceamur in venando ad similitudinem bellicae disciplinae, et utamur domitis et condocefactis,[46] ut elephantis, multaque ex earum corporibus remedia morbis et vulneribus eligamus, sicut ex quibusdam stirpibus et herbis, quarum utilitates longinqui temporis usu et periclitatione percepimus.

9. Totam licet animis tamquam oculis lustrare terram mariaque omnia: cernes jam spatia frugifera atque immensa camporum vestitusque densissimos montium, pecudum pastus, tum incredibili cursus maritimos celeritate. Nec vero supra terram, sed etiam in inti-

mis ejus tenebris plurimarum rerum latet utilitas, quae ad usum hominum orta ab hominibus solis invenitur. —*id De Naturâ Deorum*, ii. 62–64.

v. *The Heavens declare a Creator.*

1. Praeclare ergo Aristoteles: 'Si essent,' inquit, 'qui sub terra semper habitavissent [39] bonis et illustribus domiciliis, quae essent ornata signis atque picturis, instructaque rebus iis omnibus quibus [20] abundant ii qui beati putantur, nec tamen exissent umquam supra terram, accepissent autem fama et auditione, esse [41] quoddam numen et vim deorum; deinde aliquo tempore, patefactis terrae faucibus, [47] ex illis abditis sedibus evadere in haec loca, quae nos incolimus, atque exire potuissent: cum repente terram et maria caelumque vidissent, nubium magnitudinem ventorumque vim cognovissent, adspexissentque solem, ejusque tum magnitudinem pulchritudinemque, tum etiam efficientiam cognovissent, quod [44] is diem efficeret toto caelo luce [47] diffusa; cum autem terras nox opacasset, tum caelum totum cernerent astris distinctum et ornatum, lunaeque luminum varietatem tum crescentis [46] tum senescentis, eorumque omnium ortus et occasus, atque in omni aeternitate ratos immutabilesque cursus; haec cum viderent, profecto et esse deos et haec tanta opera deorum esse arbitrarentur.'—*id*. ii. 37.

vi. *An Active Old Age.*

1. Nihil [13] necesse est mihi de me ipso dicere, quamquam est id quidem senile, aetatique nostrae conceditur. Videtisne ut apud Homerum saepissime Nestor de virtutibus suis praedicet? [45] Tertiam enim jam aetatem hominum vivebat, nec erat ei verendum ne vera prae-

dicans de se nimis videretur [42] aut insolens aut loquax. Etenim, ut ait Homerus, *ex ejus lingua melle* [10] *dulcior fluebat oratio*, quam ad suavitatem nullis egebat corporis viribus.[18] Et tamen dux ille Graeciae nusquam optat ut Ajacis[6] similīs habeat decem, sed ut Nestoris; quod si sibi acciderit,[39] non dubitat quin brevi sit [46] Troja peritura.

2. Sed redeo ad me. Quartum ago annum et octogesimum Vellem [27] equidem idem posse gloriari quod Cyrus: sed tamen hoc queo dicere: non me quidem iis esse viribus quibus aut miles bello Punico, aut quaestor eodem bello, aut consul in Hispania fuerim, aut quadrienno [12] post, cum tribunus militaris depugnavi [35] apud Thermopylas M'. Glabrione consule [47]; sed tamen, ut vos videtis, non plane me enervavit, non adflixit senectus; non curia virīs meas desiderat, non rostra, non amici, non clientes, non hospites. Nec enim umquam sum adsensus veteri illi laudatoque proverbio, quod monet *mature fieri senem, si diu velis*[39] *senex esse:* ego vero me minus diu senem esse mallem,[27] quam esse senem ante quam essem. Itaque nemo adhuc convenire me voluit, cui fuerim [38] occupatus. — *id. De Senect.* 10.

INDEX OF CONSTRUCTIONS.

A. *Cases as Objects of Verbs.*
1. Object Accusative (§ 52, 1. *a, b*).
2. Two Accusatives (id. 2).
3. Dative: Indirect Object (§ 51, 1, 2).
4. Object Genitive (§ 50, 4).
5. Ablative with UTOR (§ 54, 6. *d*).

B. *Cases modifying Adjectives.*
6. Genitive (§ 50, 3. *b, c, d*).
7. Dative of Nearness (§ 51, 6).
8. Ablative of Want (§ 54, 1. *c, d*).
9.   ,,   of Source (id. 2. *a*).
10.   ,,   of Comparison (id. 5).
11.   ,,   of Means (id. 6. *c*).
12.   ,,   of Difference (id. *e*).

C. *Cases: Miscellaneous.*
13. Adverbial Accusative (§ 52, 3).
14. Accus. of Exclamation (§ 54, 4).
15. Dative of Possession (§ 51, 3).
16.   ,,   of Service (id. 5).
17.   ,,   of Reference (id. 7).
18. Ablative of Separation (§ 54, 1).
19.   ,,   of Cause (id. 3).
20.   ,,   of Means (id. 6).
21.   ,,   of Quality (id. 7).
22.   ,,   of Price (id. 8).
23.   ,,   of Specification (id. 9).
24.   ,,   Locative (id. 10).
25. Predicate Genitive (§ 50, 1. *c, d*).
26. Time and Space (§ 55, 1, 3).

D. *Moods and Tenses.*
27. Subjunctive (independent: § 57, 2-6; § 60, 2).
28. Historical Infinitive (§ 57, 8. *h*).
29. Sequence of Tenses (§ 58, 9, 10).

E. *Subordinate Constructions.*
30. Conditional Clauses (§ 59, 1).
31. Disguised Conditions (§ 60, 1).
32. Conditional Particles (§ 61, 1).
33. Temporal Clauses (§ 62, 2).
34. UBI, POSTQUAM, &c. (id. 1. *a*).
35. CUM Temporal (id. 2. *b*).
36. CUM Causal (id. 2. *e*).
37. Purpose (§ 64, 1).
38. Result (characteristic: § 65, 2).
39. Dependent Clauses (§ 66, 1, 2; § 67, 1).

F. *Substantive Clauses.*
40. Classification (§ 70, 1).
41. Accusative and Infinitive (id. 2).
42. Clauses of Purpose (id. 3).
43. Clauses of Result (id. 4).
44. Clauses with QUOD (id. 5).
45. Indirect Questions (§ 67, 2).

G. *Participial Constructions.*
46. Predicate Use (§ 72, 3).
47. Ablative Absolute (§ 54, 10. *b*).
48. Gerundive Constructions (§ 72, 5. *c*; § 73, 2).

NOTES.

LESSON 7. — 2. **habet**, *contains* or *includes*. — 4. **e**, *of* (§ 50, 2, *e*, R¹). — 10. **incommodis** (abl.), *at*.

LESS. 10. — 13. **fruges** is in apposition with **alimenta**, object of **ministrat**.

LESS. 11. — 1. **Gallicis**: supply **aedificiis**. — **remissioribus frigoribus**, *with less intense seasons of cold* (cold snaps). — 2. **quotannis singula milia**, *a thousand every year*.

LESS. 12. — 8. Understand by **vigil**, "the cock that crows in the morn." — **cantum** is governed by **nuntiant**, supplied from the preceding clause.

LESS. 14. — 1. **insula**: supply **est**, which is very often omitted in Latin. — **alter**, here *one*, corresponding to **inferior** below which is equal to another **alter**. — 4. **volcanum in cornu**, i. e. *a horn lantern*. — 8. **falsi**, *deceived*, i. e. *mistaken*. The *inconsistent things* (**res**) are **voluptatem** and **præmia**, etc., which are in apposition with **res**. — 12. **testes**, *witness:* plural because Philippi (the name of the place) happens to be plural. — **quorum** depends on **humus**. — 13. **quot homines**, etc.: the Latin form of the proverb, *many men, many minds*.

LESS. 15. — 1. **agnae meae**, in English, *of my lambs*, or *lambs of mine*. — 2. **senos**, take with **dies**.

LESS. 19. — 1. **Pausanias** was a king of Spain, victorious at Platæa, afterwards accused of taking bribes from the Persians. — 2. **qui**: the antecedent, **idem**, should be taken first in translation. In Latin the relative usually comes first, and we must look farther on for the antecedent. — 4. **nudus** is predicate. — 5. **ipse** is in agreement with the implied subject of **pugna** (**tu**). — 8. **secundis** agrees with **rebus**. Very often in Latin some word comes between an adjective and its noun on purpose to separate them; though here it is on account of metre.

LESS. 20. — 3. **hic**, *here* (adv.). — 6. **dispari domino**: the dative here is by an old or poetic use; the syntax would regularly require **a** or **ab**; **dominare** is second person singular of the verb used as passive. It has usually an active force. — 7. **mutantur**, not *are changed*, but *change* (themselves) *constantly*.

LESS. 21. — 5. **jam**, i. e. *now at length*. — 9. **de vestra vita**, *for your lives:* the usual meaning of **de** with words of fighting.

LESS. 22. — 8. **provinciam** (predicate), *as his province*.

LESS. 23. — 6. **rem**, etc. = *you have hit the nail on the head*. — 14. **illius viri** = *that great man*.

LESS. 25. — 11. **gallinis**, dative following **supponimus**, *under hens*.

LESS. 26. — 6. **licere putat**, *thinks it to be allowed:* the subject does not appear because the verb is impersonal. — 7. **ferunt**, *they say*.

Notes.

SELECTION I. — 1. **sonus** is limited by **ferri**, and subject of **reddebatur.**

2. **inhabitantibus** (dative), translate *by* (strictly *on the part of*). — **vigiliam**, object of **sequebatur**. In English the passive construction would be more natural: *watching was followed by, &c.* — **causis**, *than the cause of it* (the fear). — **solitudine**, *to solitude.* The Latin often uses the ablative to denote the penalty. — **tota**, i. e. *entirely.* — **proscribebatur**: the imperfect means not *it was advertised*, but *the advertisement was kept up.* — **seu . . . vellet**, *in case any one should wish.*

3. **quia** gives the reason of **percontatus**. — **audita** is taken with **simulacra**.

4. **ubique**, i. e. *everywhere else.* — **stabat**: the imperfect describes the appearance of the phantom.

5. **capiti**, *over the head.* — **catenis**: translate as accusative, *rattled the chains*, noticing the difference of idiom. — **idem**, governed by **innuentem**. — **quod prius**, i. e. **innuerat**. — **nec**, *and not;* as it is very often, much oftener than *nor.* — **desertus**, i. e. after he was thus abandoned. — **signum**, in apposition with **herbas**, etc., *as a mark.*

6. **quae corpus reliquerat**, i. e. *which had been left by the body* (its decay). — **exesa**, i. e. by rust. — **conditis manibus**, *the ghost being laid.* — **caruit**, *was relieved*, i. e. of the disturbance which is implied by the whole of the preceding.

SELECTION II. — 1. **otiandi** depends on **causā**. — **quod cum**, *and when this* (§ 45, 6). — **Canio**, dative following **licere**, *that Canius might use them.*

2. **qui esset** = *inasmuch as he was.* — **apparatum**, sć. **est**, *was got ready.*

3. **tantumne**, *such a quantity:* the **ne** only continues the question. — **gravate**, i. e. **agebat**, a kind of idiom. — **quid multa**, i. e. **dicam**: another common idiom, which should be noticed as such. — **impetrat**, i. e. his request. — **instructos**, agreeing with **hortos**. — **nomina facit**, *makes out the bill* (so used on account of the name in the account-book).

4. **scalmum nullum**, i. e. *not so much as a thole-pin.* — **eos nullos**, *none of them*, a regular Latin idiom. — **nullae**, sc. **feriae**. — **quod**, *so far as* (adverb accusative).

5. **aliud . . . aliud**, *one thing . . . another.*

SELECTION III. — 1. **constat**, *is made out from* (lit. *holds together*). — **hoc . . . persuasum est**, *are persuaded of this.* Notice the idiom, which is regular. — **quam eandem**, etc., *the same whom they call.*

SELECTION IV. — 1. **ea**, antecedent of **quae**, coming last, as usual in Latin. — **serendi** depends on **scientia**.

5. **se** refers to **terga**. — **latitudines**, plural (as often in Latin) because he is thinking of many cases or examples. — **fissione**, etc.: the early time when the ground had to be broken, and of course cattle were more necessary. — **aureo**, i. e. the golden age. — **fabricarier**: formerly the infinitive passive ended as here (an extract from an old poet) in er. — **manu**, connected with **vinctum**. — **vesci**, subj. of **haberetur**.

6. **longum est**: we should say in English *it would take too long* (see Gr. § 60, 2, *c*). — **pro sale**, *instead of salt*, i. e. merely to keep it from spoiling (**ne putesceret**). — **pecude** depends on **fecundius**.

7. **Pronoea**, *Providence*, in our modern sense; an idea of the Stoics, one of whom is here speaking, hence **nostra**. — **Epicurea** (pred.), *an Epicurean;* fem. on account of the gender of **Pronoea**. The idea is that Providence seems to be an Epicurean in providing so many good things for the appetite.

8. **stirpibus**, *bushes*, that have stems. — **herbis**, *plants*, grasses and the like without woody stems.

9. **licet**, *you may*, taken with **lustrare**. — **plurimarum**, etc., *very many things of use* (lit. *the usefulness of many things*).

SELECTION V. — **essent**, the subject is the implied antecedent of **qui**, *men who*. — **quoddam**, *a*. This word is used because the thing, though only referred to indefinitely, is however definitely known. — **esse deos**, *that there are gods*.

SELECTION VI. — 1. **senile**, *characteristic of old men*. — **praedicet**, from **praedico**, āre. — **aetatem**, Gr. § 52, 1. *b*. — **quam** belongs with **suavitatem**: the relative is often displaced in this way by a preposition connected with it. — **dux ille**, Agamemnon, the chief of the Trojan expedition.

2. **equidem**: the force of this word is concessive. The idea is, "though I cannot make the same boast that Cyrus (I wish I could), still this I can say, &c." The Latin particles have just this kind of force, and we cannot begin too soon to notice them. — **quidem**, again concessive (see preceding note). Translate *though I have not, &c., still* (**sed tamen**). — **ego**: notice that it is emphatic, — *I for my part.* Do not get the habit of disregarding the pronouns when expressed, because the English idiom expresses them.

VOCABULARY.

I.

ENGLISH AND LATIN.

NOTE. — The small figures denote the Conjugation of the Verbs; the letters in parenthesis, the Gender of the Nouns.

A (a certain), *quidam.*
abundance, *copia, ae* (F.).
advantage, *utilitas, atis* (F.).
advantageous, *utilis, e.*
Æneas, *Aeneas, ae* (M.).
age, *aetas, atis* (F.).
alarmed, *territus, a, um.*
Alexander, *Alexander, dri* (M.).
all (every), *omnis, e;* (whole), *totus, a, um;* all things, *omnia.*
also, *quoque, etiam.*
among, *inter* (acc.).
am, see be.
ancient, *antiquus, a, um.*
and, *et, atque, ac, -que.*
anger, *ira, ae* (F.).
animal, *animal, alis* (N.).
another, *alius;* (other of two), *alter* (§ 16, 1. *b*).
any, *ullus* (§ 16, 1. *b*); (anybody, emphatic), *quivis;* (interrog.), *num quis.*
apparel, *vestitus, ūs* (M.).
appear, *videor,*[2] *appareo.*[2]
appearance, *species, ei* (F.).
approve, *probo.*[1]
are, sign of present tense in plural.
arms, *arma, orum* (N.).
army, *exercitus, ūs* (M.).
arrangement, *dispositio, onis* (F.).
as, *ut;* as .. as, *tam .. quam;* such .. as, *talis .. qualis* (§ 22).
aside (in compos.), *se-,* as *sevoco,* call aside.

asp, *aspis, idis* (F.).
assembly, *conventus, ūs* (M.).
at (locative, see § 55, 3. *c, d*); (on account of, on occasion of), *ad* (acc.).
at last, see last.
Athens, *Athenae, arum* (F.).
Athenian, *Atheniensis, -is.*
Atlas, *Atlas, antis* (M.).
attempt (verb), *conor;*[1] (noun), *conatus, ūs* (M.).
attention, *opera, ae* (F.).
Augustus, *Augustus, i* (M.).
axle, *axis, is* (F.).

B.

bad, *malus, a, um,* (people) *improbi.*
barbarian, *barbarus, a, um.*
barbarous, *immanis, e.*
be, *sum, esse, fui.*
bearded, *barbatus, a, um.*
before, *ante* (acc.).
behalf, in behalf of, *pro* (abl.); in his own behalf, *pro se.*
betrothed, *sponsus, a, um.*
better, *melior, us;* the larger the better, *quo major eo melior.*
Bias, *Bias, antis* (M.).
bind, *vincio.*[4]
bitterness, *acerbitas, atis* (F.).
blessing, *bonum, i* (N.).
blooming, *florens, tis.*

bond, *vinculum, i* (N.).
book, *liber, bri* (M.).
border, *finis, is* (M.).
both, *ambo* (§ 18, 1. *b*), *uterque;* on both sides, *utrimque;* both .. and, *et .. et.*
bound, *finio.*[4]
boy, *puer, eri* (M.).
bramble-thicket, *dumetum, ti* (N.).
brave, *fortis, e.*
bravely, *fortiter.*
breadth, *latitudo, inis* (F.).
breaking, *fractura, ae* (F.).
brevity, *brevitas, atis* (F.).
brightness, *claritas, atis* (F.).
broken piece, *fragmentum, ti* (N.).
burdensome, *gravis;* less burdensome, *levior, us.*
but, *sed, autem* (§ 43, 3. *b*).
by (agent, after passives), *a, ab;* by no means, *nullo modo;* by night, *noctu;* by day, *interdiu.*

C.

Cæsar, *Caesar, aris* (M.).
Caius, *Gaius, i* (M.).
call, *voco.*[1]
camp, *castra, orum* (N. plur.).
can, *possum, posse, potui.*
Cannæ, *Cannae, arum* (F. plur).
carry, *porto.*[1]
cat, *felis, is* (M.).
Cato, *Cato, onis* (M.).
certain (a), *quidam.*
chain, *catena, ae* (F.).
change, *versura, ae* (F.).
changeable, *mutabilis, e.*
charge, *crimen, inis* (N.).
charm (verb), *delecto.*[1]
chest, *arca, ae* (F.).
children, *liberi, orum* (M.).
citadel, *arx, arcis* (F.).
citizen, *civis, is* (M.).
city, *urbs, urbis* (F.).
Codrus, *Codrus, i* (M.).
come, *venio.*[4]
comedy, *comoedia, ae* (F.).

commend, *commendo.*[1]
commerce, *mercatura, ae* (F.).
compare, *comparo.*[1]
confess, *fateor.*[2]
conquer, *vinco.*[3]
consent, *consensus.*
conspicuous (be conspicuous), *emineo.*[2]
conspirator, *conjurator, oris* (M.).
conspire, *conjuro.*[1]
Corcyra, *Corcyra, ae* (F.).
could, *possum* (past tenses).
countenance, *vultus, us* (M.).
country (opp. to city), *rus, ruris* (N.); (native), *patria, ae* (F.).
court, *colo.*[3]
cover, *tego.*[3]
covering (means of), *tegmentum, i* (N.).
crash, *fragor, oris* (M).
creature, *animal, alis* (N.).
crocodile, *crocodilus, i* (M.).
cure, *remedium, i* (N.).
custom, *mos, moris* (M.).

D.

danger, *periculum, i* (N.).
dated, *datus, a, um,* of a letter (lit., given to the messenger).
daughter, *filia, ae* (F.).
day, *dies, ei* (M. § 13, 2. N.); by day, *interdiu;* in one day, *uno die.*
dear, *carus, a, um.*
deceitful, *fallax, acis.*
decree, *decretum, i* (N.).
defence (means of), *munimentum, i* (N.).
delay, *mora, ae* (F.).
delight (transitive), *delecto;*[1] (intransitive), *gaudeo.*[2]
deny, *recuso.*[1]
disaster, *clades, is* (F.).
discussion, *disputatio, onis* (F.).
do (auxiliary in questions or commands), not translated.
doe, *cerva, ae* (F.).
dog, *canis, is* (M.; gen. pl., *-um*).

Vocabulary: English and Latin.

doubtful, *dubius, a, um.*
doubtless, *sane.*
dove-cote, *columbarium, i* (F.).

E.

ear, *auris, is* (F.).
early, *priscus, a, um.*
easily, *facile;* more easily, *facilius.*
end, *finis, is* (M.).
endure, *tolero.*[1]
enemy, *hostis, is* (M.).
Ennius, *Ennius, i* (M.).
equal, *par, paris.*
Ethiopians, *Aethiopes, um.*
even, *et, etiam;* not even, *ne . . quidem.*
every, *omnis, e.*
everything, *omnia, ium* (N. plur.).
eye (a little), *ocellus, i* (M.).

F.

fall, *cado.*[3]
farmer, *agricola, ae* (M.).
father, *pater, tris* (M.).
fatherland, *patria, ae* (F.).
fault, *vitium, i* (M.).
fear (as verb), *timeo,*[2] *metuo;*[3] (as noun), *timor, oris* (M.).
fertile, *fertilis, e.*
fight, *pugno.*[1]
fighting (they are), *pugnant.*
fire, *ignis, is* (M.).
fish, *piscis, is* (M.).
five, *quinque.*
flattery, *assentatio, onis* (F.).
flock, *pecus, oris* (N.).
flower, *flos, floris* (M).
flowers (made of), *floreus, a, um.*
for (conj.), *nam, enim;* (prep.) expressed by dative.
follow, *sequor, i, secutus.*
footstep, *vestigium, i* (N.).
force, *vis* (§ 11, iii. 4); (army), *copiae, arum* (F. plur.).

foreign, *externus.*
foreigner, *peregrinus, a, um* (M.).
forgetful, *oblitus, a, um.*
fortify, *munio.*[2]
fortune, *fortuna, ae* (F.).
fourth, *quartus, a, um.*
free, *liber, era, erum.*
frequent, *frequens, tis.*
friend, *amicus, i* (M.).
friendship, *amicitia, ae* (F.).
frighten, *terreo.*[2]
frog, *rana, ae* (F.).
from (away from), *a, ab;* (out of), *e, ex;* (denoting cause), expressed by ablative.

G.

Galba, *Galba, ae* (M.).
Gallus, *Gallus, i* (M.).
garb, *habitus, us* (M.).
gate, *porta, ae* (F.).
gathering, *conventus, us* (M.).
Gaul (country), *Gallia, ae* (F.); (people), *Gallus, i* (M.).
Germany, *Germania, ae* (F.).
get together, *comparo.*[1]
gift, *donum, i* (N.).
give, *do.*[1]
glad, *laetus, a, um.*
go, *eo, ire* (§ 37, 6); go away, *abeo.*
going to, expressed by future participle.
god, *deus, i* (M. § 10, 4. *f*).
gold, *aurum, i* (N.).
good, *bonus, a, um* (§ 17, 2).
goose, *anser, eris* (M.).
great, *magnus, a, um* (§ 17, 2).
greatness, *magnitudo, inis* (F.).
guard, *custos, odis* (M.).

H.

hand, *manus, us* (F.).
Hannibal, *Hannibal, alis* (M.).
have, *habeo.*[2]
hawk, *accipiter, tris* (M.).
he, *is, ille;* implied in 3d person.

healthful, *salubris, e.*
hear, *audio.*[4]
heart, *cor, cordis* (N.).
helm, *gubernaculum, i* (N.).
hence, *hinc.*
her, *ejus;* her own (refl.), *suus, a, um;* (emph.), *ipsius.*
hide, *celo.*[1]
highest, *summus, a, um.*
himself (emph.), *ipse;* (reflex.), *se.*
his, *ejus,* gen. of *is,* he; his own (refl.), *suus, a, um;* (emph.), *ipsius:* omitted where it is implied from the context.
hold *teneo.*[8]
holding (power of), *capacitas, atis* (F.).
hope (for), *spero;*[1] (noun) *spes, ei* (F).
horns (with), *cornutus, a, um.*
horse, *equus, i* (M.).
hotly, *acriter.*
house, *domus, ūs* (F. § 12, 3. e).
how great, *quantus, a, um.*
hundred (one), *centum.*

I

I, *ego* (§ 19, 1).
ibis, *ibis, is;* (or *ibidis;* F.).
Ides, *idus, uum* (F.).
implore, *imploro.*[1]
in, *in* (abl.), sometimes by ablative alone.
inconstant, *levis, e.*
into, *in* (acc.).
it, see he: it is, *est.*
Italy, *Italia, ae* (F.).

J

joining, *junctura, ae* (F.).
journey, *iter, itineris* (N.).
June, (of) *Junius, a, um* (adj.).
Juno, *Juno, onis* (F.).

K

king, *rex, regis* (M.).

L

labor, *labor, oris* (M.).
land (native), *patria, ae* (F.).
large, *magnus, a, um* (§ 17, 2).
last, *ultimus, a, um;* at last, *demum.*
Latin, *Latinus, a, um.*
lay aside, *depono.*[3]
lead, *duco.*[3]
leader, *dux, ducis* (M.).
learn, *disco.*[3]
learned, *doctus, a, um.*
length, *longitudo, inis* (F.).
less, *minor, minus.*
letter, *epistola, ae;* letters (literature), *litterae, arum* (F.).
liberty, *libertas, atis* (F.).
lie (speak falsely), *mentior.*[4]
log, *lignum, i* (N.).
longer (time), *diutius;* no longer, *non jam.* [(M.).]
love, *amo;*[1] (noun), *amor, oris*

M

maiden, *puella, ae* (F.).
maintain (keep), *teneo,*[2] (hold an opinion), *disputo.*[1] [7].
make, *facio;*[3] passive, *fio* (§ 37,
man, *vir, viri* (M.); (person), *homo, inis;* (a little), *homunculus, i* (M.); (in general), expressed by masculine adjective.
many, *multi, ae, a.*
march, *iter, itineris* (M.).
March (of), *Martius, a, um* (adj.).
Marcus, *Marcus, i* (M.).
Marius, *Marius, i* (M.).
may, *licet* (impers. § 39, *d*); (in purpose clauses), *ut* with subj.; of wish, present subj.

means (by no), *nullo modo*.
measure, *metior;*[4] (noun), *modus, i* (M.); (a little), *modulus, i* (M.).
meeting, *conventus, ūs* (M.).
Mercury, *Mercurius, i* (M.).
mighty, *magnus, a, um*.
mild (to grow), *mitesco.*[3]
mind, *animus, i* (M.).
mindful, *memor, oris*.
mingling, *mixtura, ae* (F.).
misery, *miseria, ae* (F.).
Mithridates, *Mithridates, is* (M.).
more, sign of comparative.
most, sign of superlative; *maxime*.
mourn, *lugeo*.[2]
mournful, *tristis, e*.
much, *multum;* (degree of difference) *multo*.
must, participle in *dus*.

N.

nation, *gens, gentis; natio, onis* (F.).
native land, } *patria, ae* (F.).
native city,
near, *prope*.
neighbor, *proximus, a, um*.
neither (of two), *neuter* (§ 16, I. *b*); neither .. nor, *nec .. nec* (*neque*).
new, *novus, a, um*.
night, *nox, noctis* (F.); by night, *noctu*.
nightly, *nocturnus, a, um*.
no (adj.), *nullus, a, um* (§ 16, I. *b*); no one, *nemo, inis* (M.).
noise, *strepitus, ūs* (M.).
nor, *neque, nec* (see **neither**).
north wind, *Aquilo, onis* (M.).
nose (with a large), *naso, onis* (M.).
not, *non;* interrogative, *nonne*.
nothing, *nihil* (indecl.), *nihilum, i* (N.).
now, *nunc;* (already), *jam*.
number, *numerus, i* (M.).

O.

ocean, *oceanus, i* (M.).
of, expressed by genitive; (of separation), by ablative.
often, *saepe;* very often, *saepissime*.
old, *vetus, eris;* (man or men), *senex, senis* (M.).
old age, *senectus, utis* (F.).
old man, *senex, senis* (M.).
omen, *omen, inis* (M.).
on, *in* (abl.); (of time), ablative; also where the thing *on* which is the instrument.
one (opposed to many), *unus, a, um* (§ 16, I. *b*); any one, *quis;* one .. another, *alius .. alius;* one .. the other, *alter .. alter;* no one, *nemo*.
open, *apertus, a, um;* verb, *aperio*.[4]
opportunity, *opportunitas, tatis* (F.).
other, *alius;* (of two), *alter* (§ 16, I. *b*).
our, *noster, tra, trum*.
ourselves (emphatic), *ipsi* (with 1st person plur. of verb); (reflex.), *nos*.
own, *proprius, a, um;* or gen. of *ipse*.
ox, *bos, bovis* (§ 11, iii. 4)

P.

pattern (a little), *formula, ae* (F.).
peace, *pax, pacis* (F.).
people, *populus, i* (M.); common people, *plebs, plebis* (F.).
peril, *periculum, i* (N.).
Philip, *Philippus, i* (M.).
physician, *medicus, i* (M.).
plaything, *ludibrium, i* (N.).
please, *placeo*.[2]
pleasing, *gratus, a, um*.
point, *locus, i* (M.).
politics, *res publica*.

possession (take .. of), *occupo*.¹
powers, *vires*, pl. of *vis*, *vis* (F.).
praise, *laudo*.¹
precept, *praeceptum, i* (F.).
prepare, *paro*.¹
Priam (son of), *Priamides, is* (M.).
prisoner, *captivus, i* (M.).
protection, *fides, ei* (F.).
proconsul, *proconsul, is* (M.).
prove, *probo*.¹
puppy (a little), *catellus, i* (M.).
put on, *induo*.³

Q.

quarrel, *rixa, ae* (F.).

R.

rampart, *vallum, i* (N.).
rarely, *raro*.
reach, *pervenio*.⁴
recall, *revoco*.¹
receive, *accipio*.¹
reckoning, *ratio, onis* (F.).
region, *locus, i* (F.).
reign, *regno*.¹
remedy, *remedium, i* (N.).
reply, *respondeo*.²
rich, *dives, itis*.
right, *jus, juris* (N.).
right hand, *dextra* (*dextera*), *ae* (F.).
river, *flumen, inis* (N.).
Roman, *Romanus, a, um*.
Rome, *Roma, ae* (F.).
royal, *regius, a, um*.

S.

Sabine woman, *Sabina, ae* (F.).
sacred, *sacer, cra, crum*.
sad, *tristis, e*.
sage, *sapiens, tis*.
save, *servo*.¹
scream, *clamo*.¹
sea, *mare, is* (N.).
see, *video*.²
seem, *videor*.²
self (emph.), *ipse, a, um*; (reflexive), *se*.
senate, *senatus, ūs* (M.).
serious, *severus, a, um*; *gravis, e*.
seriousness, *severitas, atis* (F.); *gravitas, atis* (F.).
Servius, *Servius, i* (M.).
set out, *proficiscor*.³
shall, sign of future tense.
sharer, *particeps, ipis*.
sheep, *ovis, is* (F.).
shepherd, *pastor, oris* (M.).
ship, *navis, is* (F.); (belonging to), *navalis, e*.
shoulder, *humerus, i* (M.).
Sicily, *Sicilia, ae* (G.).
sickly, *morbidus, a, um*.
sides (on both), *utrimque*; (on all), *undique*.
silence, *silentium, i* (N.).
silly, *stultus, a, um*.
silver, *argentum, i* (M.).
sinewy, *nervosus, a, um*.
sing, *cano*.³
Sirens, *Sirenes, um* (F.).
six, *sex*; six hundred, *sexcenti, ae, a*.
slave, *servus, i* (M.).
slay, *interficio*.³
small, *parvus, a, um* (§ 17, 12).
snowy, *nivosus, a, um*.
so, *ita, sic*; so great, *tantus*; so many, *tot*; so, as, *tam, quam*.
softness, *mollitia, ae* (F.).
soldier, *miles, itis* (M.); (belonging to a soldier), *militaris, e*.
some time, *aliquando*; (duration), *aliquamdiu*.
son, *filius, i* (M.).
song, *cantus, ūs* (M.).
sound (general), *sonus, i* (M.); (sound of voice), *vox, vocis* (F.); *sonitus, ūs* (M.; as of arms, &c.).
Southeast wind, *Notus, i* (M.).
speak, *loquor*.³
spirited, *fortis, e*.
state, *civitas, atis* (F.).

stir up, *cieo.*²
Stoic, *Stoicus, i* (M.).
strength (physical), *vires, ium* (F. plur.).
strong, *validus, a, um.*
Suevi, *Suevi, orum* (M.).
suffer, *patior, i, passus.*
Sulla, *Sulla, ae* (M.).
superstitious, *superstitiosus, a, um.*
support (means of), *columen, inis* (N.).
sure, *certus, a, um.*
sweet, *dulcis, suavis, e.*
sweetness, *suavitas, atis* (F.).
sword, *gladius, i* (F.).

T.

teach, *doceo.*²
teaching (means of), *documentum, i* (N.).
ten, *decem.*
than, *quam,* with same case following as preceding; or ablative following comparative.
that, *ille, a, um.*
themselves (emphatic), *ipsi, ae, a*; (reflex.), *se.*
there, *ibi*; there is, *est*; is there, *estne.*
they, see he.
thing, *res, rei* (F.); good things, *bona.*
think, *puto.*¹
third, *tertius, a, um.*
thirteen, *tredecim.*
this, *hic, haec, hoc* (§ 20).
those, *illi, ae, a* (§ 20, 2. *b, c, d*).
thousand, *mille* (§ 18, 1. *c*).
three, *tres, tria.*
time, *tempus, oris* (N.); — times, see § 18, 3; for some time, *aliquamdiu.*
timorous, *pavidus, a, um.*
to (of motion), *ad* (acc.); (of relation), expressed by dative; (before a verb), by the infinitive.
tray, *ferculum, i* (N.).

treat, *curo.*¹
tree, *arbor, oris* (F.).
trophy, *tropaeum, i* (N.).
true, *verus, a, um.*
truth, *veritas, atis* (F.).
try, *experior,*⁴*iri, expertus.*
trying (means of), *experimentum, i* (M.).
Tullius, *Tullius, i* (M.).
twenty, *viginti.*
twice, *bis.*
two, *duo* (§ 18, 1. *b*); two each, *bini, ae, a.*

U.

Ulysses, *Ulixes, is* or *i* (M.).
uncertain, *incertus, a, um.*
uneasy, *sollicitus, a, um.*
untimely, *immaturus, a, um.*

V.

valiant, *strenuus, a, um.*
very, expressed by superlative.
vice, *vitium, i* (N.).
victorious, *victor, oris* (M.); *victrix, icis* (F.).
victory, *victoria, ae* (F.).
violent, *violens, tis.*
virtue, *virtus, utis* (F.).

W.

wake, *vigilo.*¹
war, *bellum, i* (N.).
we, *nos* (§ 19, 1).
weep, *fleo.*²
what? *quid?*
whatever, *quicquid.*
when, *ubi.*
where, *ubi.*
whirl, *torqueo.*²
who, which (relative), *qui, quae, quod.*
who, what (interrogative), *quis* (*qui*), *quae, quod* (*quid*).
wild, *ferus, a, um.*

will, *voluntas, atis* (F.); (verb), *volo, velle, volui*.
wind, *ventus, i* (M.).
wisdom, *sapientia, ae* (F.).
wish, *volo, velle, volui; cupio*.[3]
with, *cum*; sign of ablative; with me, *mecum*.
without, *sine* (abl.).
wolf, *lupus, i* (M.).
woman, *mulier, eris* (F.).
worship, *colo*.[3]
wrong (do), *pecco*.[1]
wrong (is done), impersonal passive.

Y.

year, *annus, i* (M.).
you (sing.), *tu;* (plur.), *vos* (§ 19, 1.).
your (of one person), *tuus, a, um;* (of many), *vester, tra, trum*.
young man, *juvenis, is* (M.); *adulescens, tis* (M.).

II.

LATIN AND ENGLISH.

ā, ab (abl.), *from, away from, by;* in compos., *away, off.*
abdo,³ dere, didi, ditum, *put away, hide.*
abeo, īre, ii, itum, *go away.*
abfero (aufero), ferre, tuli, lātum, *bear away.*
ābicio³ (abjicio), icere, jēci, jectum, *throw away, cast down.*
abies, etis (F.), *fir-tree.*
abripio,³ [rapio], ripere, ripui, reptum, *snatch or dray away.*
abscēdo,³ cēdere, cessi, cessum, *move off, withdraw.*
absēns, tis (part. of absum), *absent.*
absentia, ae (F.), *absence.*
absolvo,³ solvere, solvi, solūtum, *relieve of an obligation or burden, pay off, complete.*
abundo,¹ āre, āvi, ātum, *overflow, abound.*
āc (atque), *and, as.*
accido,³ [cado], cidere, cidi, cāsum, *befell, happen.*
accipio,³ [capio], cipere, cēpi, ceptum, *take in, receive, accept.*
accipiter, tris (M.), *hawk.*
ācer, ācris, ācre, *sharp, eager.*
Achradina, ae (F.), *Achradina, a quarter of Syracuse.*
acidulus, a, um, *rather sour.*
acidus, a, um, *sour.*
ācriter (ācrius, ācerrimē), *sharply, eagerly.*
acus, ūs, F., *needle.*
ad (acc.), *to, at, towards, about* (to the number of), *for;* in compos. *in, upon, to, with.*
adeo, īre, ii, itum, *go to, approach.*
adfero, ferre, tuli, lātum, *bear to, bring.*
adficio³ (afficio), *produce in, affect with.*

adflīgo,³ flīgere, flīxi, flīctum, *dash against.*
adhūc, *hitherto, till now.*
aditus, ūs (M.), *access, approach, entrance.*
admīror,¹ āri, ātus, *wonder at, admire.*
admodum, *to a degree, quite, very.*
adsentior,⁴ sentīri, sēnsus, *agree with, assent to.*
adspicio,³ spicere. spexi, spectum, *look at, view.*
adūlātio, ōnis, (F.), *fawning, flattery.*
advento,¹ āre, *come to, approach.*
adversus (acc.), *turned towards, against.*
adversus, a, um, *turned to, opposite, in front.*
adverto,³ vertere, verti, versum, *turn to;* animum adverto, *turn the mind to, notice.*
advesperāsco,³ [vesper], ere, *approach evening, to grow late.*
aedēs, is, (F.), *temple;* plur., *house.*
aedificium, i (N.), *building, edifice.*
aedifico,¹ āre, āvi, ātum, *build, erect.*
aequo,¹ āre, āvi, ātum, *make equal.*
aequus, a, um, *level, even, equal, just.*
aerumna, ae (F.), *sorrow, grief.*
aerumnōsus, a, um, *full of grief, wretched.*
aestimo,¹ āre, āvi, ātum, *value, esteem, reckon.*
aetās, ātis (F.), *age, period of life.*
aeternitās, ātis (F.), *eternity, immortality.*
Aetna, ae (F.), *Mount Etna.*

aevum, i (N.), *age, period, lapse of time.*
afficio³ [ad, facio], facere, fēci, fectum: see adficio.
ager, agri (M.), *field.*
agito,¹ āre, āvi, ātum, *drive, move, stir, agitate, pass.*
agna, ae (F.), *ewe-lamb.*
agnosco,³ noscere, nōvi, nitum, *recognize.*
ago,³ agere, ēgi, actum, *lead, drive.*
agricola, ae (M.), *farmer.*
āio (defect. § 38, 2. *a*), *say, say yes, assert.*
Ajāx, ācis (M.), *Ajax,* a Grecian hero.
āla, ae (F.), *wing.*
alacritās, ātis (F.), *activity, eagerness, alacrity.*
albeo,² ēre, ui, *be white.*
albus, a, um, *white* (dead white).
ālea, ae (F.), *die* (of a pair of dice), *hazard.*
āles, itis (C.), *winged creature, bird.*
Alesia, ae (F.), *Alesia,* a city of Gaul.
aliēnus, a, um, *belonging to another, foreign.*
āliger, gera, *winged.*
alimentum, i (N.), *food;* pl. *kinds of food.*
aliquando, *at some time, sometimes, at length.*
aliquis, qua, quod, or quid (G. p. 48), *some, some one.*
alius, a, ud (Gr. p. 34), *other, another;* al...al, *one..another.*
alo,³ alere, alui, alitum, *feed, keep* (of animals).
altāria, ium (N.), plur., *altars.*
alter, tera, terum (Gr. p. 34), *other* (of two), *second, the other;* alter..alter, *the one, the other.*
altitūdo, dinis (F.), *height, depth.*
altus, a, um, *high, deep.*
alumnus, i (M.), *foster-child.*
amāns, tis, *loving, fond.*
ambitūs, ūs (M.), *circuit, going around.*

ambulo,¹ āre, āvi, ātum, *walk.*
āmēns, tis, *distracted, insane, frantic* (of horses).
amicitia, ae (F.), *friendship.*
amīcus, a, um, *friendly, fond; a friend.*
amo,¹ āre, āvi, ātum, *love.*
Amphitruo, onis (M.), *Amphitruo,* husband of Alcmena, the mother of Hercules.
amplitūdo, inis (F.), *fulness, grandeur.*
amplus, a, um, *full, abundant, grand, large.*
amputo,¹ āre, āvi, ātum, *prune away, cut off.*
anas, anatis (M.), *duck.*
ancilla, ae (F.), *handmaid* (Fem. of servus, *slave*).
angulus, i (M.), *corner.*
anima, ae (F.), *breath, life.*
animadverto³ [animum adverto], vertere, verti, versum, *perceive* (accusative).
animus, i (M.), *mind, soul, courage;* animum adverto, *perceive.*
annivesārius, a, um, *yearly.*
annōna, ae (F.), *the grain-crop, grain* (in market), *price of grain.*
annus, i (M.), *year.*
ante (acc.), *before* (prep. and adv.); ante..quam, *before* (rel. adv.); non ante... quam, *not...until.*
antiquus, a, um, *ancient.*
apage (def. § 38, 2. *f*), *away! begone!*
aperio,⁴ īri, ui, apertum, *open.*
apertus, a, um (part. of preceding), *opened, open.*
apiārium, i (N.), *bee-house, apiary.*
apis, is (F.), *bee.*
Apollo, inis (M.), *Apollo,* god of music and art.
appāreo,² ēre, ui, *appear.*
apparo,¹ āre, āvi, ātum, *make ready.*
appello,¹ āre, āvi, ātum, *call.*
Appius, i (M.), *Appius* (Claudius), a man's name.

aptus, a, um, *fitted, fit.*
apud (acc.), *at, near, among, with, in* (of authors).
Apulia, ae (F.), *Apulia,* the South East part of Italy.
aqua, ae (F.), *water, spring.*
aquātio, ōnis (F.), *watering-place.*
aquila, ae (F.), *eagle* (the Roman standard).
Aquillius, i (M.), a proper name.
Aquilo, ōnis (M.), *Aquilo* (the North wind), *the North.*
arātor, ōris (M.), *ploughman.*
arātrum, i (N.), *plough.*
arbitror,[1] āri, ātus, *judge, think, suppose.*
arbor (ōs), ŏris (F.), *tree.*
arbustum, i (N.), *orchard.*
ardēns, tis (participle of ardeo), *blazing.*
ardeo,[2] ēre, arsi, arsum, *blaze, burn.*
area, ae (F.), *open space, area, court-yard.*
argentārius, a, um, *pertaining to silver or money;* argentārius, *a money lender;* argentāria (sc. res), *banking business.*
argentum, i (N.), *silver.*
Aristotelēs, is (M.), *Aristotle,* a Greek philosopher.
arma, ōrum (N.), *arms, weapons;* ad arma, *to war;* in armīs, *under arms.*
armātus, a, um, *armed.*
aro,[1] āre, āvi, ātum, *plough.*
ars, artis (F.), *art, skill.*
artē (tius, tissimē), *closely.*
artifex, ficis (M.), *artist, artisan, workman.*
asinus, i (M.), *ass, donkey.*
asper, era, erum, *rough, harsh, sharp.*
aspernor,[1] āri, ātus, *spurn, scorn.*
aspis, idis (F.), *asp* (a poisonous serpent).
asporto[1] [abs, porto], āre, āvi, ātum, *carry off.*
astrum, i (N.), *star, heavenly body.*
at, *but, but yet, still.*
Athēnae, ārum, *Athens,* the most famous city of Greece.

Athēnodōrus, i (M.), a proper name.
Atlantiadēs, is (M.), *descendant of Atlas* (Mercury).
Atlās, antis (M.), *Atlas,* a Titan, changed to a mountain.
atque (ac.), *and, as, and even.*
Atreus, i (M.), *Atreus,* father of Agamemnon.
Atrīdēs, is (M.), *son of Atreus.*
attendo,[3] dere, di, tum, *stretch towards.*
attingo[3] [tango], tingere, tigi, tactum, *touch upon, touch, reach.*
audeo,[2] audēre, ausus sum, *dare, venture.*
audio,[4] īre, īvi, ītum, *hear.*
audītio, ōnis (F.), *hearsay.*
aufero [ab, fero], auferre, abstuli, ablātum, *bear away, remove.*
augeo,[3] augēre, auxi, auctum, *increase.*
augur, uris (M.), *augur* (interpreter of omens).
auguror,[1] āri, ātus, *interpret omens, interpret, predict.*
aureus, a, um, *golden, of gold.*
aurīga, ae (M.), *driver, charioteer.*
auris, is (F.), *ear.*
aurītus, a, um, *having ears.*
aurum, i (N.), *gold.*
ausus, a, um (part. of audeo).
aut, *or;* aut . . . aut, *either . . . or.*
autem, *but, however, now, moreover.*
auxilium, i (N.), *aid, help.*
avāritia, ae (F.), *avarice, greed.*
avārus, a, um, *greedy, avaricious.*
avis, is (F.), *bird.*
axis, is (M.), *axle, axis* (of the earth).

B.

Babylōn, ōnis (F.), *Babylon.*
barba, ae (F.), *beard.*
barbarus, a, um, *barbarian.*

beātus, a, um, *blessed, happy, wealthy.*
bellicōsus, a, um, *warlike.*
bellicus, a, um, *warlike.*
bellum, i (N.), *war.*
belua, ae (F.), *beast, monster, strange animal.*
bene, *well.*
benefacio, facere, fēci, factum; pass. benefīo, *do good, benefit.*
bestia, ae (F.), *animal, beast, brute.*
biennium, i (N.), *two years* (period of).
bis, *twice.*
bonus, a, um, *good, kind, fine.*
bōs, bovis (Gr. p. 22; C.), *ox, cow;* plur. *cattle.*
brevis, e, *short;* brevi, *in a short time.*
Britannia, ae (F.), *Britain.*

C.

C, initial for *Gaius* (*Caius*). The spelling Gaius is the correct one, but need not be preserved in English.
cado,[3] cadere, cecidi, cāsum, *fall.*
Caecilius, i (M.), *Caecilius*, a family name.
caedo,[3] caedere, cecīdi, caesum, *fell, cut down, kill, beat.*
caelum, i (N.); pl. caeli, ōrum, (M.), *sky, heaven.*
Caesar, aris (M.), *Cæsar.*
caleo,[2] ēre, ui, *be hot* or *warm.*
calesco,[3] ere, *grow hot* or *warm.*
campus, i (M.), *field, plain.*
candēns (part. of candeo), tis, *glowing, hot.*
canis, is (M.; gen. pl. um), *dog.*
Canius, i (M.), a proper name.
Cannae, ārum (F.), *Cannæ*, a town in S. E. Italy, when the Romans were defeated by Hannibal, B. C. 216.
cano,[3] ere, cecini, cantum, *sing, sound, play.*

cantillo,[1] āre, *sing feebly, chirp, warble.*
Cantium, i (N.), *Kent,* the S. E. part of Britain.
canto,[1] āre, āvi, ātum, *sing.*
cantus, ūs (M.), *song, chant, music.*
capāx, ācis, *capacious, roomy.*
capesso,[3] ere, ivi, ītum, *take hold of, seize, grasp.*
capillus, i (M.), *hair.*
capio,[3] ere, cēpi, captum, *take, catch.*
caput, capitis (N.), *head.*
careo,[2] ēre, ui, *lack, be free, be relieved* (of annoyance, p. 64), *do without.*
cāritās, ātis (F.), *dearness,* both as *affection* and as *high price.*
carmen, inis (N.), *song.*
caro, carnis (F.), *flesh, meat.*
castanea, ae (F.), *chestnut.*
castra, ōrum (N. pl.), *camp.*
catellus, i (M.), *little puppy.*
catēna, ae (F.), *chain.*
Catilīna, ae (M.), proper name.
catulus, i (M.), *whelp, puppy.*
causa, ae (F.), *cause, motive, care;* causā, *for the sake of.*
cēdo,[3] ere, cessi, cessum, *move, move away, yield, retire, resign.*
celeber, bris, bre, *thronged, celebrated, numerous.*
celeritās, ātis (F.), *swiftness.*
cēlo,[1] āre, āvi, ātum (with acc.), *hide, cover.*
cēna, ae (F.), *dinner.*
cēno,[1] āre, āvi, ātum, *dine, sup.*
cēnsor, ōris (M.), *censor* (a Roman officer).
centēsimus, a, um, *hundredth.*
centum, *a hundred.*
cēra, ae (F.), *wax;* pl. *wax tablets* (for writing).
Ceres, eris (F.), *Ceres*, goddess of grain.
cerno,[3] -ere, -crēvi, -crētum, *distinguish, descry, decide.*
certē, *surely, at any rate.*
certō, *certainly.*

Vocabulary: Latin and English.

certo,¹ āre, āvi, ātum, *decide, strive, contend.*
certus, a, um (part. of cerno), *decided, certain, sure.*
cervix, īcis (F.; generally plur.), *neck, shoulders.*
cervus, i (M.), *stag.*
cesso,¹ āre, āvi, ātum, *cease.*
[cēterus], a, um (masc. sing. not used), *other, the rest.*
Chrysippus, i (M.), *Chrysippus,* a Stoic philosopher.
cibus, i (M.), *food.*
cicāda, ae (F.), *tree-locust, katydid.*
Cicero, ōnis (M.), *Cicero.*
circā, *about.*
circum (acc.), *about, around.*
circumcīdo,³ ere, cīdi, cīsum, *cut* or *trim around.*
circumcīsus, a, um, *cut off all around.*
circumplico,¹ āre, āvi, ātum, *fold round, wrap round, surround.*
clādēs, is (F.), *massacre, loss.*
clārus, a, um, *bright, famous, loud.*
Claudius, i, *Claudius,* a Roman family name.
cliēns, tis (C.), *client, dependent.*
coctilis, e, *baked.*
coepi (def. Gr. p. 81), *began.*
cōgito,¹ āre, āvi, ātum, *think, reflect.*
cognātio, ōnis (F.), *relationship* (by blood).
cognōmen, inis (N.), *surname, family name.*
cognosco,³ ere, nōvi, nitum, *learn, recognize, know.*
collēga, ae (M.), *colleague.*
collego,³ ere, lexi, lectum, *gather, collect.*
colligo,¹ āre, āvi, ātum, *bind together.*
colo,³ ere, colui, cultum, *cherish, till, worship.*
comes, itis (C.), *companion.*
commemoro,¹ āre, āvi, ātum, *call to mind, relate, recount.*
commīlito, ōnis (M.), *fellow-soldier, comrade.*
commoditās, ātis (F.), *convenience, advantage.*
commoveo,² ēre, mōvi, mōtum, *move, disturb* (violently).
commūnis, e, *common.*
compes, edis (F.), *fetter.*
complector,³ ti, plexus, *embrace.*
complūrēs, ia, *very many.*
comprobo,¹ āre, āvi, ātum, *make good, prove, verify.*
computo,¹ āre, āvi, ātum, *reckon, compute.*
concēdo,³ ere, cēssi, cēssum, *allow.*
concerpo,³ [con, carpo], ere, cerpsi, cerptum, *pluck, gather.*
concilio,¹ āre, āvi, ātum, *win, call together, unite, conciliate.*
concilium, i (N.), *council.*
concito,¹ āre, āvi, ātum, *rouse, excite* (strongly).
conclamatum incendium, *a cry of fire* (lit. *fire cried*).
conclāmo,¹ āre, āvi, ātum, *cry aloud.*
conclūdo³ [con, claudo], ere, clūsi, clūsum, *shut up.*
conclūsus, a, um (part. of last), *shut up.*
concutio⁸ [con, quatio], ere, cussi, cussum, *shake, clash, shatter, rattle.*
condemno,¹ āre, āvi, ātum, *condemn.*
condo,³ dere, didi, ditum, *put together, found, build, put to rest, get in, cure* (of crops).
condocefactus, a, um, *trained, tamed.*
condūco,³ ere, xi, ctum, *bring together, hire.*
cōnfectus, a, um (part. of conficio), *wrought, reduced.*
cōnfero, ferre, tuli, lātum, *bring together, compare, betake* (one's self).
cōnficio,³ ere, fēci, fectum, *make thoroughly, finish, prepare* (make up).

cōnfirmo,[1] āre, āvi, ātum, *confirm, strengthen, affirm.*
cōnfiteor,[2] ēri, fessus, *confess, acknowledge, admit.*
conjunx, jugis (C.), *partner,* i.e., *husband* or *wife.*
conjūrātio, ōnis (F.), *conspiracy.*
conquīro[3] [con. quaero], ere, quīsīvi, quīsītum, *enquire, search out.*
cōnsecro,[1] āre, āvi, ātum, *consecrate.*
cōnsequor,[3] sequi, secūtus, *follow close, overtake, attain.*
cōnsilium, i (N.), *counsel, plan, wise counsel, wisdom.*
cōnsimilis, e, *very like, just like.*
cōnsto,[1] stāre, stiti, stātum, *consist, be established.*
cōnsul, ulis (M.), *consul* (Roman officer).
contendo,[3] ere, di, tum or sum, *stretch towards, strive, contend;* contendo ab, *urge upon.*
contexo,[3] ere, ui, xtum, *weave together.*
continēns, tis (part. of contineo), *continuous;* as a noun, *the continent.*
contineo,[2] ēre, tinui, tentum [con, teneo], *hold together, contain, keep.*
contrā, as prep. (acc.), *against, over against;* as adv., *on the other hand.*
convenio,[4] īre, vēni, ventum, *meet.*
conventus, ūs (M.), *meeting, concourse.*
converto,[3] ere, ti, sum, *turn.*
convoco,[1] āre, āvi, ātum, *call together.*
convīvium, i (N.), *feast, banquet.*
cōpia, ae (F.), *abundance, opportunity;* plural, *forces.*
cōpiōsus, a, um, *abounding in resources.*
cor, cordis (N.), *heart.*
cornicen, cinis (M.) [cornu, cano], *horn-blower.*
cornū, ūs (ū) (N.), *horn.*

corpus, ŏris (N.), *body.*
corruptus, a, um (part. of conrumpo), *spoiled, corrupt.*
Cotta, ae (M.), a Roman surname.
crās, *to morrow.*
crāstinus, a, um, *belonging to the morrow;* crāstinus (sc. dies) i (M.), *the morrow.*
crēber, bra, brum, *thick, close, frequent.*
crēbresco,[1] ere, crebui, *grow dense, thicken, increase.*
crēdo,[3] dere, didi, ditum, *trust, believe.*
creo,[1] āre, āvi, ātum, *create, elect.*
crepitus, ūs (M.), *noise* (rattling), *din.*
cresco,[3] ere, crēvi, crētum, *grow, increase.*
Crēta, ae (F.), *Crete,* an island.
crēta, ae (F.), *chalk.*
crētāceus, a, um, *of chalk.*
Crētēnsis, e, *belonging to Crete.*
crocodīlus, i (M.), *crocodile.*
crucio,[1] āre, āvi, ātum, *torment, torture.*
crūdēlis, e, *bloody, cruel.*
crūdēlitās, ātis (F.), *cruelty.*
crūs, crūris (N.), *leg.*
culpa, ae (F.), *fault.*
cultrīx, īcis (F.) [colo], *she that tills,* &c.
cultus, ūs (M.), *tillage, worship, mode of living, attention.*
cum (prep. abl.), *with;* cum (adv.), *when;* cum primum, *as soon as;* cum . . tum, *while . . so also.*
cunābulum, i (N.), *cradle.*
cupiditās, ātis (F.), *eager desire, cupidity.*
cupidus, a, um, *eager, desirous, greedy.*
cur, *why.*
cūra, ae (F.), *care, anxiety.*
cūrātio, ōnis (F.), *cure, treatment.*
cūria, ae (F.), *senate house.*
currus, ūs (M.), *chariot, car.*
cursus, ūs (M.), *running, course, race, voyage.*

custōdia, ae (F.), *custody, guard, guarding.*
custōdio,[4] īre, īvi, ītum, *guard.*
custōs, ōdis (M.), *guard, guardian.*
cymba, ae (F.), *boat.*
Cyrus, i (M.), *Cyrus,* a Persian king (proper name).

D.

damno,[1] āre, āvi, ātum, *condemn.*
Dardanus, i (M.), *Dardanus,* a man's name.
dē (abl.), *down from, of, about.*
dea, ae (F.), *goddess.*
decem, *ten.*
decemvir, viri (M.), *decemvir* (one of a board of ten).
decimus, a, um, *tenth.*
dēclāro,[1] āre, āvi, ātum, *make clear, show, declare.*
dēflecto,[3] ere, flexi, flexum, *bend, turn off* (down or away).
deinde, *then.* [*please.*
dēlecto,[1] āre, āvi, ātum, *delight,*
dēleo,[2] ēre, ēvi, ētum, *blot out, destroy, annihilate.*
dēlicātus, a, um, *delicate, effeminate.*
dēmentia, ae (F.), *madness, folly.*
dēmeto,[3] ere, messui, messum, *reap.*
dēnique, *at length, in short.*
dēpugno,[1] āre, āvi, ātum, *fight* (out a battle).
dēnsus, a, um, *crowded, dense, close.*
dēsero,[3] ere, dēserui, dēsertum, *forsake, desert.*
dēsīdero,[1] āre, āvi, ātum, *lack, want, desire, feel the want of.*
dēsīlio[4] [de, salio], īre, silui, sultum, *leap down.*
dēsino,[3] ere, dēsii, dēsitum, *leave off, cease.*
dexter, tera (tra), terum (trum), *right, right hand.*
deus, i (M.; § 10, 4 *f*), *a god, divinity.*

dīco,[3] ere, dīxi, dīctum, *say, tell.*
dictito,[1] āre, *keep saying, repeat.*
diēs, diēi (M. rarely F.), *day.*
difficilis, e, *difficult.*
diffundo,[3] ere, fūdi, fūsum, *pour far and wide, pour out, spread.*
digitus, i (M.), *finger, toe.*
dignus, a, um, *worthy* (followed by abl.)
dīlābor,[3] i, lāpsus, *fall apart, glide away.*
dīligo,[3] ere, lexi, lectum, *love* (less strong than amo).
dīmitto,[3] ere, mīsi, missum, *send away, dismiss.*
Dion, ōnis (M.), *Dion,* a patriot of Sicily.
dīrectus, a, um (part. of **dīrigo**), *straight, perpendicular.*
dīreptio, ōnis (F.), *plundering.*
dīrus, a, um, *dreadful.*
Dis, Dītis, *Pluto,* god of the Lower World.
dis (in comp.), *apart.*
disciplīna, ae (F.), *system of teaching, discipline, training.*
discipulus, i (M.), *scholar, disciple.*
dispar, paris, *unequal, unlike.*
distinctus, a, um (part. of **distinguo**), *set off, studded.*
diū, diūtius, diūtissimē, *long* (of time).
diūturnus, a, um, *long* (in time), *lasting, durable, long continued.*
dīversor,[1] āri, ātus, *turn aside.*
dīversōrium, i (N.), *inn, tavern.*
dīversus, a, um, *inconsistent.*
dīvēs, itis, *rich.*
dīvīnus, a, um, *divine, godlike, superhuman.*
do,[1] dāre, dēdi, dātum, *give;* (in comp.), *place, give birth to.*
doceo,[2] ēre, docui, doctum, *teach, tell* (followed by two acc.)
doleo,[2] ēre, dolui, *be painful, feel pain, grieve, suffer* (with abl. of that from which one suffers).
dolor, ōris (M.), *pain, grief.*
dolus, i (M.), *trick, fraud, craft.*
domicilium, i (N.), *home, residence.*

domino,[1] āre, āvi, ātum, *rule, be master of* (old Latin, for the later **dominor**, deponent).
dominus, i (M.), *master, lord.*
domo,[1] āre, domui, domitum, *subdue, tame, break in.*
domus, ūs (F. § 12, 3. e), *house;* domi, *at home.*
dōnec, *until.*
dubito,[1] āre, āvi, ātum, (with quin), *doubt;* (with infin.), *hesitate.*
dūco,[3] ere, dūxi, dūctum, *lead.*
dulcis, e, *sweet, fresh* (of water).
duo (Gr. p. 42), *two.*
dūro,[1] āre, āvi, ātum, *endure, last, hold out.*
dūrus, a, um, *hard, hardy.*
dux, ducis (M.), *leader, guide.*

E.

ē (ex), *from, out of;* in comp., *out, completely.*
edāx, ācis, *greedy.*
ēditus, a, um (part. of **ēdo**), *prominent.*
ēdo,[3] ere, ēdidi, ēditum, *put forth, give out, produce.*
edo, edere or esse, ēdi, ēsum (Gr. p. 80), *eat.*
effero, ferre, extuli, ēlātum, *carry out, carry away.*
efficientia, ae (F.), *efficacy, potency.*
efficio[3] [ex, facio], ere, fēci, fectum, *make out, effect.*
effigiēs, iēi (F.), *image, apparition.*
effodio,[3] ere, fōdi, fossum, *dig up.*
effugio,[3] ere, fūgi, fugitum, *escape from.*
egēns, tis (part. of **egeo**), *destitute.*
egeo,[2] ēre, egui, *need.*
ego, mei (Gr. p. 44), *I.*
egomet (Gr. p. 44), *I myself.*
ēgregius, a, um, *excellent, distinguished, unusual, fine, remarkable.*

ēlātus, a, um (part. of **effero**), *carried away.*
ēlegantia, ae (F.), *elegance.*
elementum, i (N.), *beginning.*
elephantus, i (M.), *elephant.*
ēligo,[3] ere, ēlexi, ēlectum, *pick out, elect, select, choose.*
ēloquentia, ae (F.), *eloquence.*
emo,[3] ere, ēmi, emptum, *buy* (originally *take*).
empturio,[4] īre, *want to buy.*
ēnervo,[1] āre, āvi, ātum, *enervate, unman.*
enim, *for.*
Ennius, i (M.), *Ennius,* an early poet of Rome.
ēnsis, is (M.), *sword* (poetic).
eo, *thither.*
eō .. quō (with comparatives, § 22, c), *the .. the.*
eo, īre, īvi, itum (Gr. p. 80), *go.*
Epicūrēus, a, um (belonging to Epicurus), *Epicurean.*
eques, itis (M.), *rider, horseman, knight, gentleman;* pl. *cavalry.*
equester, tris, tre (*belonging to horsemen*), *of cavalry.*
equidem, *in fact, for my part* (concessive), *it is true, to be sure.*
equus, i (M.), *horse.*
ergō, *therefore, then.*
ēripio,[3] ere, ripui, reptum, *snatch away, rescue.*
erro,[1] āre, āvi, ātum, *wander, err, stray.*
ērumpo,[3] ere, ērūpi, ēruptum, *break out, burst forth.*
esca, ae (F.), *food.*
esse (see **sum**), *to be.*
et, *and, even;* et .. et, *both .. and, on the one hand .. on the other.*
etenim, *for* (you see, you know, &c.)
etiam, *also, even, yes.*
ēvādo,[3] ere, di, sum, *come out, escape, pass out.*
ex, *out of, from, of.*
exclāmo,[1] āre, āvi, ātum, *cry out, exclaim.*

Vocabulary: Latin and English.

exclūdo,[3] [ex, claudo], clūdere, clūsi, clūsum, *shut out, hatch.*
exedo,[3] ere, ēdi, ēsum, *eat out, consume, wear away.*
exemplum, i (N.), *sample, pattern, example.*
exeo, īre, ii, itum, *go forth.*
exerceo,[2] cēre, cui, citum, *keep busy* (lit. drive out), *manage;* (in passive), *train one's self.*
exercitus, ūs (M.), *army.*
exēsus, see exedo.
exorior,[4] īri, ortus, *arise.*
expello,[3] ere, puli, pulsum, *drive out.*
expulsor, ōris (M.), *expeller.*
exsisto,[3] ere, stiti, stitum, *arise, appear, exist.*
exspecto,[1] āre, āvi, ātum, *look out for, expect, wait.*
exstinguo,[3] ere, nxi, nctum (poke out), *extinguish, destroy.*
exsto,[1] stāre, stiti, stitum, *stand forth, rise.*
externus, a, um, *foreign;* (noun), *stranger.*
extrā (acc.), *outside of, beyond.*
extraho,[3] ere, traxi, tractum, *draw out, drag.*
extrēmus, a, um, *last;* extrema insula, *the end of the island.*

F.

fabricor,[1] āri, ātus, *manufacture, fabricate, forge.*
fabricārier, old infinitive of preceding = fabricāri.
fābula, ae (F.), *fable, tale.*
facile, *easily.*
facilis, e, *easy.*
facio,[3] ere, fēci, factum, *make, do.*
fāgus, i (F.), *beech-tree.*
fallo,[3] ere, fefelli, falsum, *deceive.*
falsus, a, um (part. of fallo), *deceived, false.*
fāma, ae (F.), *common talk, report, fame.*
familia, ae (F.), *household, family.*

familiāris, e, *belonging to a family, familiar;* (noun), *friend.*
Fannius, i (M.), proper name.
fātum, i (N.), *fate, destiny.*
faucēs, ium (F.), *jaws, throat, passage* (into any thing).
fax, facis (F.), *torch, firebrand.*
fēcundus, a, um, *fertile, productive, prolific.*
fēlis, is (M.), *cat.*
fera, ae (fem. of ferus), *wild creature, wild animal, or beast.*
fere, *almost, for the most part, about.*
fēriae, ārum (F.), *holiday.*
fero, ferre, tuli, lātum, *bear, carry, tell.*
ferreus, a, um, *of iron.*
ferrum, i (N.), *iron.*
ferus, a, um, *wild, fierce.*
fessus, a, um, *weary.*
festus, a, um, *festal.*
fētus, a, um, *producing, full, prolific.*
Fidēnae, ārum, *Fidenæ* (an Italian town).
Fidēnās, ātis, *of Fidenæ.*
fidēs, is (F.), *string;* (plur.), *lyre.*
fidēs, ei (F.), *faith.*
fidus, a, um, *faithful.*
figūra, ae (F.), *figure, shape.*
figūro,[1] āre, āvi, ātum, *fashion, shape.*
fīlia, ae (F.), *daughter.*
fīliola, ae (F.), *little daughter.*
fīliolus, i (M.), *little son.*
fīlius, i (M.), *son.*
fingo,[3] ere, finxi, fictum, *fashion, form, imagine.*
fio, fieri, factus (Gr. p. 80), *become, be made, be done.*
fissio, ōnis (F.), *cleft, cleaving.*
flagrāns, tis, *blazing.*
flamma, ae (F.), *blaze, flame.*
flōreo,[2] ēre, ui, *flourish, bloom.*
flōresco,[3] ere, *begin to bloom.*
flōs, flōris (M.), *flower.*
flūmen, inis (N.), *stream, river.*
fluo,[3] ere, fluxi, fluxum, *flow.*
folium, i (N.), *leaf.*
fōns, fontis (M.), *spring, fountain.*

forma, ae (F.), *inward form (organization), form, shape.*
formica, ae (F.), *ant.*
formido, inis (F.), *dread, terror.*
fortis, e, *sturdy, strong, brave.*
formula, ae (F.), *little model, pattern, rule, formula, writ* (legal).
fortiter, *bravely.*
fortūna, ae (F.), *fortune.*
forum, i (N.), *forum* (public square).
fossa, ae (F.), *ditch, trench.*
foveo,² ēre, fōvi, fōtum, *warm, fondle, cherish, brood over.*
fragilis, e, *frail, easily broken.*
fragor, ōris (M.), *crash,* (crashing) *noise.*
frango,³ ere, frēgi, fractum, *break.*
frāter, tris (M.), *brother.*
frīgus, ōris (N.), *cold.*
frōns, dis (F.), *leaf.*
frōns, tis (F.), *brow, forehead.*
fructus, tūs (M.), *fruit* (grain), *fruits* (generally), *profit.*
frūgēs, um (F.), *grain, produce.*
frūgifer, fera, ferum, *productive.*
frūmentum, i (N.), *grain.*
fruor,³ i, fructus, *enjoy.*
fulmen, inis (N.), *thunderbolt, flash of lightning.*
fūmo,¹ āre, āvi, ātum, *smoke.*
fundo,³ ere, fūdi, fūsum, *pour, pour forth.*
fūnestus, a, um, *fatal.*
fūr, fūris (M.), *thief.*
furor, ōris (M.), *madness* (raving), *rage* (mad).
fūror,¹ āri, ātus, *steal* (by craft).
furtim (adv.), *by stealth.*
fustis, is (F.), *club.*

G.

Gāius, *Caius* (M.), a proper name, e.g. C. Laelius.
Gallia, ae (F.), *Gaul* (partly coinciding with France).
Gallicus, a, um, *of Gaul, Gallic.*
gallīna, ae (F.), *hen.*
Gallus, i (M.), *a Gaul.*

geminus, a, um, *twin.*
gener, eri (M.), *son-in-law.*
genero,¹ āre, āvi, ātum, *generate, produce.*
genetrix, trīcis (F.), *mother.*
gēns, gentis (F.), *race, nation.*
genus, eris (N.), *race, family, descent, kind, class.*
Germānus, a, um, *German.*
gero,³ ere, gessi, gestum, *carry, carry on, wear, do.*
gigno,³ ere, genui, genitum, *produce.*
Glabrio, ōnis (M.), a proper name.
gladiātor, ōris (M.), *swordsman, gladiator.*
gladiolus, i (M.), *little sword.*
gladius, i (M.), *sword.*
glaeba, ae (F.), *sod, turf* (of untilled ground).
glōria, ae (F.), *glory.*
glōrior,¹ āri, ātus, *glory, glory in* (abl.), *boast* (with accus. of a neuter pronoun).
gradus, ūs (M.), *step.*
Graecia, ae (F.), *Greece.*
Graecus, a, um, *Greek;* Graeci, pl. *the Greeks.*
grāmen, inis (N.), *grass.*
grātia, ae (F.), *favor, influence, good will;* gratiā, (with genitive), *for the sake of.*
grātiōsus, a, um, *favorite, popular.*
grātus, a, um, *pleasing.*
gravātē, *reluctantly.*
gravis, e, *heavy, weighed down.*
grex, gregis (M.), *flock, herd.*
guberno,¹ āre, āvi, ātum, *steer, govern.*
gusto,¹ āre, āvi, ātum, *taste.*
gymnasium, i (N.), *gymnasium.*

H.

habeo,² ēre, ui, itum, *hold, have, keep, imply, have in itself, consider, have for.*
habilis, e, *handy.*

habito,¹ āre, āvi, ātum, *inhabit, live.*
Hannibal, alis (M.), *Hannibal, a Carthaginian general.*
haud, *not (modifying only one word).*
Henna, ae (F.), *Enna, a vale in Sicily.*
Hennēnsis, e, *of Enna.*
Hēraclīdēs, is (M.), *a name of a philosopher.*
herba, ae (F.), *grass, turf.*
Hercynia, ae (silva), *Hercynian (a German forest).*
heri, *yesterday.*
herus, i (M.), *master* (less approved spelling for erus).
heu, *alas!*
hīc, *here.* [speaker).
hic, haec, hōc, *this* (near the
hiemps, hiemis (F.), *winter.*
hilaris, e, *cheerful.*
Hispānia, ae (F.), *Spain.*
histōria, ae (F.), *history.*
hōdiernus, a, um, *to day's;* hōdierno die, *to-day.*
Homērus, i (M.), *Homer, the Greek poet.*
homo, hominis (M.), *man* (as a human being), *person, fellow* (in contemptuous sense).
honestus, a, um, *becoming, honorable.*
honor, ōris (M.), *honor.*
horreo,² ēre, horrui, *bristle up, shudder.*
hortulus, i (M.), *little garden.*
hortus, i (M.), *garden.*
hospes, itis (M.), *host, guest.*
hospitium, i (N.), *office of host.*
hostīlis, e, *of an enemy.*
hostis, is (M.), *enemy* (public).
hūc, *hither.*
hūmānitās, ātis (F.), *courtesy, refinement, culture.*
hūmānus, a, um, *of man, human.*
humerus, i (M.), *shoulder.*
humilis, e, *low, lowly.*
humo,¹ āre, āvi, ātum, *bury.*
humus, i (F.), *ground;* humi, *on the ground.*

I

ībis, is (F.), *ibis, a sacred bird of Egypt.*
īdem, eadem, idem, *the same.*
īdōlon, i (N.; Greek noun), *image, apparition.*
igitur, *therefore.*
ignārus, a, um, *unaware, ignorant.*
ignāvia, ae (F.), *sloth, cowardice.*
ignāvus, a, um, *sluggish, cowardly.*
ignis, is (M.), *fire;* pl. (fires of the sky), *lights.*
ille, illa, illud, *that* (away from speaker).
illūstris, e, *bright, well lighted, illustrious.* [tion.
imāgo, inis (F.), *image, appari-*
imitor,¹ āri, ātus, *imitate.*
immānis, e, *monstrous.*
immemor, oris, *unmindful.*
immēnsus, a, um, *measureless, immense, unbounded.*
immo, *nay, on the contrary, nay rather.*
immūtābilis, e, *unchangeable.*
impendeo,² ēre, pendi, *overhang, threaten.*
imperātor, ōris (M.), *commander* (in chief).
imperium, i (N.), *authority, command, state* (as a power).
impero,² āre, āvi, ātum, *command, require.*
impetro,¹ āre, āvi, ātum, *accomplish, obtain* (a request).
impetus, ūs (M.), *attack, violence, impulse;* animi impetus, *impetuosity of feeling.*
implico,¹ āre, āvi, ātum, *entwine, entangle.*
improbus, a, um, *wicked, bad.*
impudēns, tis, *shameless, impudent.*
in (acc.), *into, for, towards;* (abl.), *in, in regard to.*
inānis, e, *empty, unreal.*
incendium, i (N.), *fire* (conflagration).

incendo,³ ere, di, sum, *set on fire, inflame.*
incolo,⁴ ere, colui, cultum, *inhabit.*
incommodum, i (N.), *annoyance, inconvenience, disaster* (by a euphemism).
incēdo,³ ere, cēssi, cēssum, *move on, advance.*
incrēdibilis, e, *incredible.*
incultus, a, um, *uncultivated, rude.*
incumbo,³ ere, cubui, cubitum, *lie upon, devote one's self to* (dative).
incunābulum, i (N.), *cradle.*
inde, *thence, then.*
inerro,¹ āre, āvi, ātum, *wander in or over, pass before* (dative).
infacētus, a, um, *without humor.*
infāmis, e, *ill famed, infamous.*
infēlīx, īcis, *unfruitful, unfortunate, unhappy.*
inferior, ius (comp. of inferus), *lower, inferior.*
infernus, a, um, *of the world below.*
infero, ferre, tuli, lātum, *bring in or upon;* bellum infero, *make war.*
inferus, a, um, *lower.*
infestus, a, um, *hostile, dangerous, in a dangerous condition.*
infīnītus, a, um, *unlimited, infinite, immeasurable.*
inflammo,¹ āre, āvi, ātum, *set on fire.*
ingeniōsus, a, um, *full of genius.*
ingenium, i (N.), *nature, mind, genius.*
inhabito,¹ āre, āvi, ātum, *inhabit.*
inimīcus, a, um, *unfriendly, hostile;* (as noun), *personal enemy.*
initium, i (N.), *beginning;* initio, *at first.*
injussū (abl.), *without orders* (with genitive *from*).
innātus, a, um, *inborn.*
innuo,³ ere, ui, ūtum, *nod, hint.*
innocēns, tis, *harmless, innocent.*
innocentia, ae (F.), *innocence.*

inopia, ae (F.), *want, need.*
inquam (def. Gr. p. 81), *say* (always in direct discourse and following some of the words said), *said he,* &c.
insānio,⁴ īre, īvi, ītum, *be insane.*
insānus, a, um, *not sound, insane.*
insero,³ ere, serui, sertum, *weave in, bind in.*
insero,³ ere, sēvi, situm, *implant.*
insidiae, ārum (F.), *ambush, plot.*
insitus, a, um (part. of insero).
insolēns, tis, *unused, insolent, arrogant.*
insono,² āre, sonui, sonitum, *resound over, rattle* (dative).
institor, ōris (M.), *trader* (travelling), *vender.*
instruo,³ ere, xi, ctum, *furnish.*
insula, ae (F.), *island.*
intendo,³ ere, tendi, tēnsum, *strain, devote.*
inter (acc.), *between, among;* inter sē, *with each other.*
interdiu, *by day, in the day time.*
interdum (adv.), *sometimes.*
interior, ius, *inner.*
interpellātor, ōris (M.), *interruptor;* sine interp., *without interruption.*
intimus, a, um, *inmost.*
intrā (acc.), *within.*
intus (adv.), *within.*
invenio,⁴ īre, vēni, ventum, *come upon, find.*
investigo,¹ āre, āvi, ātum, *track, trace, investigate* (following a scent).
invidia, ae (F.), *envy, jealousy.*
invīto,¹ āre, āvi, ātum, *entertain, invite.*
ipse, a, um, *self* (emphatic), *himself, herself,* &c.
irācundē (adv.), *with irascibility, with little patience.*
irācundus, a, um, *irascible, high-tempered.*
ira, ae (F.), *anger.*
is, ea, id, *he, she, it, that.*

iste, ista, istud, *that yonder, that of yours.*
ita, *so, thus.*
Italia, ae (F.), *Italy.*
itaque, *therefore, accordingly.*
item, *likewise, also.*
iterum, *again, a second time.*

J.

jaceo,² ēre, jacui, jacitum, *lie, be low, lie low.*
jacio,³ ere, jēci, jactum, *throw, cast.*
jacto,¹ āre, āvi, ātum, *cast, toss.*
jam, *now, already;* jam non, *no longer* (with present); jam vero, *then again;* (with future), *presently.*
janua, ae (F.), *doorway, door.*
jocor,¹ āvi, ātus, *jest, joke.*
Jovis, see Juppiter.
jubeo,² ēre, jussi, jussum (acc. and infin.), *order.*
jūdex, icis (M.), *judge, juror* (in plural properly *jurors*).
jūdico,¹ āre, āvi, ātum, *judge, decide.*
jugum, i (N.), *yoke, ridge* (of hill).
Julius, i (M.), *Julius*, a man's name.
Julius, a, um, *of Julius.*
Juppiter, Jovis (M.), *Jupiter*, king of the gods.
Jura, ae (M.), a mountain of Gaul.
jūs, jūris (N.), *right, privilege.*
jussū (abl.), *by command.*
juvenis, is (M.), *young man.*
juvencus, i (M.), *bullock.*
juventūs, ūtis (F.), *youth.*
juvo,¹ āre, jūvi, jūtum, *aid, help, do good, favor, please.*

K.

Karthāgo, inis (F.), *Carthage.*

L.

labor, ōris (M.), *toil, hardship.*
labōriōsē (adv.), *with great labor.*
labōriōsus, a, um, *toilsome.*
labōro,¹ āre, āvi, ātum, *toil, labor, trouble one's self.*
lāc, lactis (N.), *milk.*
lacus, cūs (M.), *lake.*
Laelia, ae (F.), proper name, daughter of C. Laelius.
laetus, a, um, *glad, blooming, gladdening* (by abundance), *abundant.*
largitās, ātis, *generosity, bounty.*
largus, a, um, *broad.*
lateo,² ēre, latui, *be hidden* (with acc.).
laterculus, i (M.), *brick.*
lātitūdo, inis (F.), *breadth.*
latrōcinium, i (N.), *robbery.*
latus, eris (N.), *side.*
lātus, a, um, *wide.*
laudātus, a, um (part. of following), *much praised.*
laudo,¹ āre, āvi, ātum, *praise.*
laus, laudis (F.), *praise.*
legātus, i (M.), *lieutenant.*
legio, ōnis (F.), *legion.*
lego,³ ere, lēgi, lectum, *read.*
legūmina, um (N.), pl. *vegetables.*
Lemannus, i (lacus), *Lake Geneva.*
lentus, a, um, *slow.*
levis, e, *light.*
levitās, ātis, *lightness.*
lēx, lēgis (F.), *law* (written).
Lībera, ae (F.), *Proserpine*, daughter of Ceres.
liber, bri (M.), *book.*
līber, era, erum, *free.*
līberātor, ōris (M.), *deliverer.*
līberē, *freely.*
līberī, ōrum (M.), *children.*
līberō,¹ āre, āvi, ātum, *set free.*
lībertās, tātis (F.), *freedom, liberty.*
licet, licuit, *it is permitted, one may.* [trance.
līmen, inis (N.), *threshold, en-*

lingua, ae (F.), *tongue.*
lis, litis (M.), *lawsuit, quarrel.*
litera, ae (F.), *letter;* plur. *epistle, literature.*
literātus, a, um, *lettered, learned.*
locuplēs, ētis, *wealthy.*
locuplēto,[1] āre, āvi, ātum, *enrich.*
locus, i (M.); plur. loca, ōrum (N.), *place, region.*
longē, ius, issimē, *far, by far, at a distance.*
longimanus, a, um, *long-handed.*
longinquus, a, um, *distant, long* (of time).
longus, a, um, *long;* longum est, *it would take too long.*
loquāx, ācis, *talkative.*
loquor,[3] i, locūtus, *speak, talk.*
lubet (or libet), *it pleases, one is glad.*
lūcidus, a, um, *bright.*
lūcus, i (M.), *grove.*
lūdus, i (M.), *play, school.*
lūmen, inis (N.), *light.*
lūna, ae (F.), *moon.*
lupus, i (M.), *wolf.*
lustro,[1] āre, āvi, ātum, *purify, survey.*
lūx, lūcis (F.), *light.*
Lysippus, i (M.), proper name.

M.

M'. abbrev. of *Manius,* a man's name.
maciēs, iēi (F.), *leanness, emaciation.*
maculo,[1] āre, āvi, ātum, *stain.*
magis, *more.*
magister, tri (M.), *master, teacher.*
magistra, ae (F.), *mistress.*
magistrātus, tūs (M.), *magistrate, office.*
Magnesia, ae (F.), a town in Asia Minor.
magnitūdo, inis (F.), *greatness, size;* incrēdibili magnitudine, *of marvellous size.*
magnus, a, um, *great* (in all senses), *powerful.*

mājusculus, *somewhat large.*
mālo, malle, malui, *wish more, choose rather.*
malus, a, um, *bad, malicious* (i. e. intended).
maneo,[2] ēre, mānsi, mānsum, *wait, stay, remain.*
mānēs, ium (M.), *a departed spirit.*
Manlius, i (M.), a proper name.
maniplāris, e, *belonging to a company, maniplary.*
maniplus, i (M.), *wisp of straw* (used as a standard for a military company), hence later the company itself.
manus, ūs (F.), *hand.*
Marcellus, i (M.), a famous Roman.
Marcus, i (M.), a Roman proper name.
mare, is (N.), *sea.*
maritimus, a, um, *of the sea, on the sea.*
māter, tris (F.), *mother.*
māteria, ae; iēs, iēi (F.), *timber, material.*
mātricīda, ae (M.), *matricide.*
mātūrē, *early, hastily.*
maximus, a, um, *greatest.*
medeor,[2] ēri, *heal.*
medicābilis, e, *curable.*
medicāmen, inis (N.), *remedy.*
medicāmentārius, a, um, *pertaining to* (dealing in) *remedies.*
medicāmentōsus, a, um, *curative.*
medicāmentum, i (N.), *remedy.*
medicīna, ae (F.), *medicine.*
medicīnālis, e, *medicinal.*
medicor,[1] āri, ātus, *heal.*
medicōsus, a, um, *curative.*
medicus, i (M.), *physician.*
meditor,[1] āri, ātus (devote one's self to), *practise, meditate.*
Mediolānum, i (N.), *Milan* (a city of North Italy).
medius, a, um, *mid, middle, middle of* (in agreement with noun).

mēl, mellis (N.), *honey.*
meminī (defect. Gr. p. 81), *remember.*
memor, oris, *mindful.*
memoria, ae (F.), *memory.*
memoro,[1] āre, āvi, ātum, *call to mind, relate.*
mēns, mentis (F.), *mind.*
mēnsūra, ae (F.), *measure.*
mentior,[4] īri, itus, *lie* (speak falsely).
mercenārius, ī (M.), *hireling.*
mercēs, ēdis, *pay, wages.*
mercēs, ium (F.), plur. *commodities, wares.*
mercor,[1] āri, ātus, *trade, buy..*
Mecurius, ī (M.), *Mercury*, god of trade, &c.
meridiēs, iēi (M.), *midday, noon, south.*
meritus, a, um (part. of mereor), *deserved.*
-met, intensive syllable added to pronouns.
metior,[4] īri, mēnsus, *measure, measure out.*
metus, ūs (M.), *apprehension, fear.*
meus, mea, meum, *my, mine.*
micō,[1] āre, micuī, *quiver, shine, glitter.*
mīles, itis (M.), *soldier.*
mīlitāris, e, *military.*
mīlitō,[1] āre, āvi, *serve* (as a soldier).
mille, plur. mīlia, *thousand.*
Minerva, ae (F.), *Minerva*, goddess of arts and wisdom.
minister, trī (M.), *attendant.*
ministra, ae (F.), *handmaid.*
ministrō,[1] āre, āvi, ātum, *serve, supply, afford.*
minor, minus, *smaller, lesser.*
minus, *less,* with adj. *not so* (much).
mīrābiliter, *wonderfully.*
mīror,[1] āri, ātus, *wonder.*
mīrus, a, um, *wonderful, marvellous;* quid mirum, *what wonder?*
miser, era, erum, *wretched.*

mītigō,[1] āre, āvi, ātum, *mellow, tame down.*
mītis, e, *mild, gentle, mellow.*
mixtūra, ae (F.), *mixture.*
Mnēsarchus, ī (M.), a proper name.
modius, e (M.), *modius*, a measure of grain.
modo (in a manner), *only, just now.*
moenia, ium (N.), *fortifications.*
mollis, e, *soft, smooth, mealy* (of fruits, &c.).
moneō,[2] ēre, uī, itum, *warn, admonish, advise.*
monitus, ūs (M), *admonition.*
mōns, montis (M.), *mountain.*
mōnstrum, ī (N.), *prodigy, monster.*
monumentum, ī (N.), *record, monument.*
mora, ae (F.), *delay.*
morbus, ī (M.), *disease.*
moribundus, a, um, *dying.*
morior,[4] īri, mortuus, *die.*
moror,[1] āri, ātus, *delay.*
mors, mortis (F.), *death.*
mortālis, e, *mortal.*
mōs, mōris (M.), *custom;* plur., also *character.*
mōtus, ūs (M.), *disturbance* (of insurrections and the like).
moveō,[2] ēre, mōvī, mōtum, *move* (in all senses).
mox, *presently.*
Mucius, ī (M.), a proper name.
mulier, eris (F.), *woman.*
multitūdō, inis (F.), *multitude, great number.*
multus, a, um (generally plural), *much, many.*
multō (adverbial ablative), *by much, much.*
mūlus, ī (M.), *mule.*
mūniō,[4] īre, īvi, ītum, *fortify.*
munusculum, ī (N.), *little gift.*
mūrus, ī (M.), *wall.*
mūs, mūris (M.), *mouse.*
mūtō,[1] āre, āvi, ātum, *change.*
myrīca, ae (F.), *heather.*
myrtus, ūs or ī (F.), *myrtle.*

N.

nam, *for.*
nanciscor,[3] ci, nactus *or* nanctus, *catch, get, find.*
nārēs, ium (M.), *nostrils, nose, scent.*
narro,[1] āre, āvi, ātum, *tell, relate, talk of* (with acc.).
nascor,[3] ci, nātus, *be born.*
Nasīca, ae (M.), *Nasica*, a name of one of the Scipios.
nātūra, ae (F.), *nature.*
nātūrālis, e, *natural.*
nātus (part. of **nascor**), a, um, *born.*
nāvigo,[1] āre, āvi, ātum, *sail, navigate.*
nāvis, is (F.), *ship.*
nē, *lest;* (with imperat.), *not;* ne .. quidem, *not .. even, not .. either;* (with subj.), *not to.*
-ne (enclitic), mark of interrogation.
Neapolis, is (F.), name of a city (Newtown).
nēc (neque), *and not, neither, nor.*
nēc enim, *for .. not* (you see).
necesse (indec.), *necessary.*
nefās, *moral wrong, impiety.*
negōtior,[1] āri, ātus, *do business.*
negōtium, i (N.), *business, task.*
nēmo, inis (M.), *no one, no* (in apposition with noun).
nemus, oris (N.), *grove.*
nerēis, idis (F.), *nereid, sea-nymph.*
Nereus, i (M.), *Nereus*, god of the sea depths.
Nestor, oris (M.), *Nestor*, a wise and aged Greek chieftain.
nihil, ind., *nothing;* (as adv.), *not at all.*
nihilum, i (N.), *nothing.*
nimis, *too, too much.*
nōbilis, e, *well known, noble, famous.*
noceo,[2] ēre, nocui, nocitum (dat.), *do harm, hurt, injure.*
nocturnus, a, um, *nightly, of the night.*

nōmen, inis (N.), *name, bill* (of exchange).
nōmino,[1] āre, āvi, ātum, *name.*
nōn, *not.*
nōndum, *not yet.*
nōnne, *not?* (in questions: *does .. not, do .. not,* &c.).
nōs, nostrum (i), nōbis (Gr. p. 44), *we.*
nosco,[3] ere, nōvi, nōtum, *learn;* perf. *know* (as an acquaintance).
nōster, tra, trum, *our, ours.*
novem, *nine;* decem novem, *nineteen.*
novus, a, um, *new.*
nox, noctis (F.), *night.*
nūbēs, is (F.), *cloud.*
nūbo,[3] ere. nūpsi, nūptum (dat.), *marry* (of the woman).
nūdus, a, um, *naked, bare, unclad* (without the outer garment).
nullus, a, um (gen. īus), *no, none.*
Numantia, ae (F.), a town in Spain.
num, sign of question expecting negative answer: translate in indirect question, *whether;* in direct, by denial and question together, *is not, is it?*
numerus, i (M.), *number.*
nūmen, inis (N.), *nod, will, divine being, divinity.*
numquam (nunquam), *never.*
nunc, *now* (emphatic).
nuntio,[1] āre, āvi, ātum, *bring news, announce, report.*
nūpta, ae (F.), *married, bride* (lit. *veiled*).
nusquam, *nowhere.*
nux, nucis (F.), *nut.*

O.

O, interjective *Oh!*
ob (acc.), *on account of.*
obfero, ferre, tuli, lātum, *bring in the way of, offer.*
obfirmo,[1] āre, āvi, ātum, *strengthen against, strengthen.*

Vocabulary: Latin and English.

oblecto,[1] āre, āvi, ātum, *delight, amuse.*
obsequium, i (N.), *indulgence (of whims), deference.*
obtingo,[3] [ob, tango], ere, tigi, tactum, *fall to the lot of any one* (dative).
occāsus, ūs (M.), *setting, west.*
occulo,[3] ere, cului, cultum, *hide.*
occultus, a, um, *hidden;* in occultō, *under cover.*
occupo,[1] āre, āvi, ātum, *seize, take possession of.*
occupātus, a, um (part. of preceding), *engaged.*
octo, *eight.*
octōgēsimus, a, um, *eightieth.*
oculus, i (M.), *eye.*
ōdium, i (N.), *hate, hatred.*
odor, ōris (M.), *smell.*
offero, see obfero.
oleum, i (N.), *olive oil, oil.*
olīvētum, i, *olive-orchard.*
Olympias, adis (F.), *Olympiad* (Greek measure of time).
Olympius, a, um, *of Olympus, Olympian,* an epithet of Jupiter.
ōmen, inis (N.), *omen.*
omnīno, *altogether, at all.*
omnis, e. *all, every;* omnia, *every thing.*
onus, eris (N.), *burden.*
opāco,[1] āre, āvi, ātum, *darken.*
opēs, opum (F.), plur., *wealth, resources.*
opifex, ficis (M.), *workman.*
opīnio, ōnis (F.), *notion, idea* (not *opinion*).
opiparis, e, *sumptuous.*
oppidum, i (N.), *town* (fortified).
oppugno,[1] āre, āvi, ātum, *attack, besiege* (in the modern sense).
[ops], opis (F.; only used as name of a goddess in the nominative; in the other cases), *help.*
opto,[1] āre, āvi, ātum, *choose, desire, wish for* (with acc.)
optimē (superl. of bene), *best.*
optimus, a, um, *best* (superl. of bonus).
opus, eris (N.), *work.*

ōrātio, ōnis (F.), *speech, oration, plea, discourse.*
orbis, is (M.), *circle, world;* orbis terrarum, *the earth.*
ordo, inis (M.), *order, rank, class.*
oriēns, tis (M.), *rising, east.*
orior, īri, ortus, *rise* (inflected in 3d conjugation).
ornātus, a, um (part. of orno), *adorned, well furnished, highly ornamented.*
ornātus, ūs (M.), *ornament.*
ōro,[4] āre, āvi, ātum, *pray, entreat, pray for.*
ortus, ūs (M.), *rising.*
ortus, a, um (part. of orior), *risen, rising, hatched.*
ōs, ōris (N.), *mouth.*
os, ossis (N.), *bone.*
oscen, inis (N.), *a bird giving omens by its note* (technical word of augury).
osculor,[1] āri, ātus, *kiss.*
ostendo,[3] ere, di, sum, *and* tum, *show.*
ostento,[1] āre, āvi, ātum, *display.*
ostium, i (N.), *door* (outer).
ōtior,[1] āri, ātus, *be idle, enjoying leisure.*
ōtium, i (N.), *leisure, ease, peace.*
ovīle, is (N.), *sheepfold.*
ovis, is (F.), *sheep.*
ōvum, i (N.), *egg.*

P.

P. for **Publius.**
paene, *almost.* [canton.
pagus (M.), i, *village, district.*
palam, *openly.*
palliolum, i (N.), *robe.*
palūs, ūdis (F.), *marsh.*
palūster, tris, tre, *marshy.*
Papirius, i (M.), *Papirius;* Papiria (F.), *Papirian,* title of a Roman law from the name of its mover.
paries, etis (M.), *wall* (of house).
pario,[3] ere, peperi, partum, *bring forth, produce.*

pariter, *equally, alike.*
paro.¹ āre, āvi, ātum, *get, prepare.*
pars, partis (F.), *part, share.*
parvus, a, um, *small.*
pascua, uum (N. plur.), *pastures.*
passus, ūs (M.), *step, pace;* mille passūs, *a mile.* [a slave).
pastor, ōris (M.), *shepherd* (usually
pastus, a, um, *fed, pastured.*
pastus, ūs (M.), *pasturage.*
patefacio,³ facere, fēci, factum, *lay open.*
pateo,² ēre, ui, *lie open.*
pater, tris (M.), *father.*
patera, ae (F.), *bowl* (sacrificial).
paternus, a, um, *of a father, of one's father.*
patria, ae (F.), *fatherland, native city or land.*
patricius, a, um, *patrician.*
patrius, a, um, *of a father, of one's native city.*
pauci, ae, a, *few, a few* (only).
paulus, a, um, *small;* paulum, *a little, a little while.*
Paulus, i (M.), *a man's name.*
pauper, eris, *poor.*
Pausaniās, ae (M.), a Spartan commander.
peculium, i (N.), *property* (private savings of a slave).
pecco,¹ āre, āvi, ātum, *do wrong.*
pecūnia, ae (F.), *money.*
pecus, udis (F.), *creature* (in a flock or herd), *domestic animal.*
pecus, oris (N.), *flock.*
penetro,¹ āre, āvi, ātum, *penetrate.*
per (acc.), *through* (also in sense by means of); *throughout* (in adverbial phrase).
peragro,¹ āre, āvi, ātum, *travel over.*
percipio³ [per, capio], ere, cēpi, ceptum, *learn, gather, gain, receive.*
percontor,¹ āri, ātus, *inquire* (particularly).
percrēbresco,³ ere, *thicken, become frequent, spread.*

peregrīnus, a, um, *foreign.*
perennis, e, *perennial.*
pereo, īre, ii, *perish;* (in the perfect), *be dead, be destroyed.*
perexcelsus, a, um, *very high.*
pergo,³ ere, perrexi, perrectum, *keep on, proceed.*
periclitātio, ōnis (F.), *trial.*
periculum, i (N.), *trial, danger.*
perpetuus, a, um, *perpetual, eternal.*
Persa, ae (M.), *Persa,* a name (of a dog); also the same as *Perses,* name of a king.
persequor,³ sequi, secūtus, *pursue, follow out.*
Persēs, sis (M.), *Perses,* a king of Macedonia.
persuādeo,² ēre, suāsi, suāsum, *persuade.*
pertineo,² ēre, tinui, tentum, *reach, extend;* pertineo ad, *belong to, have to do with.*
perverto,³ ere, ti, sum, *overturn, overthrow.*
pes, pedis (M.), *foot* (also as a measure).
pestilēns, tis, *infected, unwholesome.*
peto.³ ere, petīvi, petītum, *aim at, seek, ask.*
Phalaris, idis (M.), *Phalaris,* a name of a tyrant.
Philippi, orum (M; plur.), the place of the battle between the assassins and the partisans of Cæsar.
philosophus, i (M.), *philosopher.*
Phoebus, i (M.), *Phoebus,* a name of Apollo.
pictūra, ae (F.), *painting, picture.*
piger, gra, grum, *sluggish, inactive.*
pingo,³ ere, pinxi, pictum, *paint.*
piscātor, ōris (M), *fisherman.*
piscis, is (M.), *fish.*
piscor,¹ āri, ātus, *fish, catch fish.*
placeo,² ēre, ui, itum, *please;* mihi placet, *I like.*
plānē, *plainly, wholly, absolutely.*
plānitiēs, iēi (F.), *plain, level.*

Plato, ōnis (M.), *Plato*, a Greek philosopher.
plausus, ūs (M.), *clapping (of hands), applause, flapping (of wings) against the side (laterum).* [*plebeian.*
plēbēius, a, um, *of the people,*
plēbs, plēbis (F.), *common people, commons.*
plēnus, a, um, *full.*
-plico,[1] āre, ui, itum (in compos.), *wrap.*
plūrimus, a, um, *most, very much* (plur.), *very many.*
plūs, plūris (comp. of **multus**; N. in sing.), *more.*
Poenus, a, um, *Carthaginian.*
poēta, ae (M.), *poet.*
polliceor,[2] ēri, itus, *promise (freely), offer.*
pōmum, i (N.), *apple, fruit.*
pōno,[3] ere, posui, positum, *leave, put, place.*
Ponticus, i (M.), *Ponticus*, name of a Greek philosopher.
populus, i (M.), *people (organized community).*
por- (in compos.), *forward.*
porta, ae (F.), *gate.*
porticus, ūs (F.), *gallery, porch, colonnade.*
porto,[1] āre, āvi, ātum, *carry.*
portus, ūs (M.), *harbor.*
posco,[3] ere, poposci, poscitum, *claim, demand, call for.*
possum, posse, potui, *can, be able;* past tenses, *could.*
post (acc.), *behind, after.*
posteā, *afterwards.*
postquam, *after, when, as soon as* (always in subordinate clause).
posterus, a, um, *later* (with dies); *next.*
posteri (plur. of preceding), *posterity.*
postrēmus, a, um (sup. of preceding), *last.*
Postumus, i, a Roman name.
postridiē, *the next day,* or *the day after.*

potestās, ātis (F.), *power (over,* with gen.).
prae (abl.), *before, in comparison with, considering.*
praeceps, cipitis [prae, caput], *headlong.*
praeceptor, ōris (M.), *instructor.*
praeceptum, i (N.), *instruction, precept.*
praecipio,[3] ere, cēpi, ceptum, *instruct* (dative).
praeclārē, *nobly, handsomely.*
praeclārus, a, um, *glorious.*
praedico,[1] āre, āvi, ātum, *tell, boast, speak of with praise.*
praedium, i (N.), *landed estate.*
praefero, ferre, tuli, lātum, *hold before, bear before, prefer* (dat.)
praemium, i (N.), *reward, prize.*
praesēns, tis (part. of **praeesse**), *present.*
praetendo,[1] ere, tendi, tentum, *hold before, close* (dative).
praeter (acc.), *beyond, besides, except.* [this).
praetereā, *besides* (lit. beside
precēs, um (F.; plur. of **prex**, not used), *prayers.*
pressus, a, um (part. of **premo**), *pressed.*
Priamidēs, is (M.), *son of Priam.*
prīmum, **prīmō**, *first, at first.*
pretium, i (N.), *price.*
princeps, cipis, *chief.*
prīmus, a, um, *first;* prīmō, *at first.*
prius, *before, sooner.*
prīvātim, *privately.*
prō (abl.), *before, for, instead,* or *in behalf of.*
prōdigium, i (N.), *prodigy.*
prōdo,[3] dere, didi, ditum, *give forth, betray.*
proelium, i (N.), *battle.*
profecto, *as a fact, surely.*
prōfero, ferre, tuli, lātum, *publish.*
proficiscor,[3] ci, profectus, *set forth.*
prōgredior,[3] di, gressus, *advance.*

prōícĭo³ (prōjicio), ere, jēci, jectum, *cast forth, throw.*
prōlēs, is (F.), *offspring.*
prōmitto,³ ere, mīsi, mīssum (let go forth), *promise.*
promissus, a, um (part. of preceding), *long.*
promptus, a, um (part. of promo), *drawn out* (from the store), *ready.*
Pronoea, ae (F.), *divine providence.*
prope (acc.), *near, near by.*
propter (acc.), *near, on account of.*
prōscrībo,³ ere, scripsi, scriptum, *post up* (in writing), *advertise.*
Prōserpina, ae (F.), *Proserpine,* daughter of Ceres, and queen of the lower world.
prōtinus (adv.), *further on.*
prōtŭli (prōfero), *put forth.*
prōverbium, i (N.), *proverb.*
prōvincia, ae (F.), *province* (sphere of action).
prōximus, a, um, *nearest, next;* e proximo, *from near by.*
prytanium, i (N.), *town hall.*
publicē, *publicly, officially, at the public expense.*
publicus, a. um, *public.*
Publius, i (M.), Roman name.
puella, ae (F.), *girl, maiden.*
puer, i (M.), *boy.*
pugillāris, e (belonging to the hand), plur. *note-book.*
pugno, ae (F.), *battle, fight.*
pugnāx, ācis, *pugnacious.*
pugna,² āre, āvi, ātum, *fight.*
pugnus, i (M.), *fist.*
pulcher. chra, chrum, *beautiful.*
pulchritūdo, inis (F.), *beauty.*
pullus, i (M.), *chicken, duckling.*
Pūnicus, a, um, *Carthaginian.*
Pyrrhus, i (M.), a king of Epirus.
pusillanimus, a, um, *feeble-hearted.*
pusillus, a. um, *feeble, slight.*
pūtesco.³ ere, ui, *grow offensive* (in smell), *rot.*

puto,¹ āre, āvi, ātum, *think.*
putrefacio,³ ere, feci, factum, *corrupt.*
putrefactus, a. um (part. of preceding), *rotted.*
Pythius, i (M.), Pythius, a man's name.

Q.

quā, *where, in what way.*
quācumque, *wherever.*
quadriennium, i (N.), (space of) *four years.*
quaero,³ ere, quaesīvī, quaesītum, *seek, ask.*
quaeso,³ ere, *ask, pray, inquire.*
quaestio, ōnis (F.), *investigation.*
quaestor, ōris. (M.), *quæstor,* Roman officer like paymaster.
quālis, e, *as, what* (correl. to tālis); tāle .. quāle, *such a thing* — as; often alone, implying its correlative, *such as.*
quam, *how, as, than.*
quamquam, *although* (lit. however), *though* (corrective).
quantus, a, um, *how great* (in all senses), *how strong,* &c.
quartus, a, um, *fourth.*
quasi, *as if, as it were.*
quatio,³ ere, *shake, rattle.*
quattuor, *four.*
-que (enclitic), *and.*
queo (def. Gr. p. 82), *can.*
qui, quae, quod, *who, which, that, as* (rel.); quod, *so far as.*
qui, old ablative form of quis; quīcum, *with whom.*
quia, *because.*
quīcumque, quaecumque, quodcumque, *whoever.*
quīdam, quaedam, quoddam, *a (certain) one.*
quidem, *in fact, to be sure, at least*; ne .. quidem, *not even* followed by sed. &c., may often be translated *though.*
quīlibet, quaelibet, quodlibet, *who you will, any (whatever).*

quin, *why not, but that.*
quīnam (quisnam), (emph. interrog.), *who* (tell me).
quintuplex, plicis, *five-fold.*
Quintus, ī (M.), Roman proper name.
quīntus, a, um, *fifth.*
Quirītēs, ium, (Roman) *citizens.*
quis, quae, quid, *who? what?*
quisquam, quaequam, quod- or quidquam, *any one* (with neg. cond. and interrog.).
quisque, quaeque, quodque, *every, each.*
quisquis (§ 21, 2), *whoever.*
quō, *whither;* with comparatives, eō .. quō, *the .. the, in proportion as.*
quoque, *also, as well.*
quot, *how many, as* (many).
quotannīs, *each or every year, yearly.*

R.

rapidus, a, um, *swift.*
rapio,[3] ere, rapuī, raptum, *seize, carry off* (with force).
rapto,[1] āre, *seize* (with violence).
raptus, a, um, *caught.*
raptus, ūs (M.), *carrying off.*
rārus, a, um, *rare.*
ratio, ōnis (F.), *reckoning, reason.*
ratus, a, um, *confirmed, fixed.*
re- or red- (in compos.), *back or again.*
recēns, tis, *recent.*
recidīvus, a, um, *restored, revived.*
recido,[3] ere, cidī, *fall back.*
redditus, a, um, *restored.*
reddo,[3] dere, didī, ditum, *give back, restore, give out, produce* (as of sounds).
reditus, ūs (M.), *return.*
redeo, īre, iī, itum, *return.*
redundo,[1] āre, āvī, ātum, *overflow.*
refero, ferre, tulī, lātum, *bring back, relate, represent, restore to* (acc.).
refervesco,[3] ere, *boil up.*
rēgīna, ae (F.), *queen, princess.*
regno,[1] āre, āvī, ātum, *reign.*
Rēgulus, ī (M.), a Roman name.
rēligio, ōnis (F.), *religion, worship, reverence.*
relinquo,[3] ere, līquī, lictum, *leave, abandon.*
reliquus, a, um, *remaining.*
remedium, ī (N.), *remedy.*
remissus, a, um, *slack, remiss;* comparative, *less intense.*
remitto,[3] ere, mīsī, missum, *send back, let go, relax.*
repente, *suddenly.*
reperio,[4] īre, reperī, repertum, *find, discover.*
repōno,[3] ere, posuī, positum, *put by, store.*
rēs, rei (F.), *thing, property, event;* (in plural), *circumstances.*
res publica, *commonwealth, public life.*
reservo,[1] āre, āvī, ātum, *reserve, keep back, preserve.*
resono,[1] āre, sonuī, sonitum, *resound.*
respicio,[3] ere, spexī, spectum, *look back.*
respondeo,[2] ēre, spondī, sponsum, *reply.*
retro, *back, backward, behind* (adv.).
revoco,[1] āre, āvī, ātum, *recall, renew* (by calling back).
rex, rēgis (M.), *king.*
rītē, *rightly, duly.*
rīvulus, ī (M.), *little stream.*
rīvus, ī (M.), *stream, brook.*
rixa, ae (F.), *brawl, quarrel.*
rogo, āre, āvī, ātum, *ask, demand, entreat.*
Rōma, ae (F.), *Rome.*
Rōmānus, a, um, *Roman.*
rostrum, ī (N.), *beak;* pl. *the platform* (the raised place from which Roman orators addressed the people).
rursus, *again.*

S.

sacer, cra, crum, *sacred.*
sacerdōs, ōtis (M. or F.), *priest, priestess.*
saepe, *often.*
saevitia, ae (F.), *cruelty.*
saevus, a, um, *cruel.*
sagācitās, ātis (F.), *keenness of scent, sagacity, keenness.*
sagāx, ācis, *keen, sagacious.*
Saguntum, i (N.), *Saguntum,* a city of Spain.
sal, salis (M.), *salt.*
salūs, ūtis (F.), *health, safety, preservation.*
salveo,[2] ēre, *be well.*
salvus, a, um, *safe and sound.*
sanguis (sanguen), inis (M.), *blood* (in the veins, or fresh), also in the sense of *stock* or *race.*
sapiēns, tis, *wise.*
sapientia, ae (F.), *wisdom.*
satis, *enough, sufficiently.*
scalmus, i (N.), *thole-pin.*
scelerātus, a, um, *guilty.*
scelus, eris (N.), *crime, guilt.*
scientia, ae (F.), *knowledge.*
scīlicet, *that is to say, forsooth* (ironical).
scio,[4] scīre, scīvi, scītum, *know* (a fact).
Scīpio, ōnis (M.), *Scipio,* a Roman name.
scrībo,[3] ere, scrīpsi, scrīptum, *write.*
sē, sui, sibi, *self* (Gr. p. 44).
semet, see -met.
sē- }
sed- } (in compos.), *apart.*
sector, ōris (M.), *divider, buyer.*
secundum (prep. acc.), *along.*
secundus, a, um, *following, second, favorable.*
secūris, is (F.), *axe.*
secūrus, a, um, *secure.*
sed, *but.*
sēdecim, *sixteen.*
sedeo,[2] ēre, sēdi, sessum, *sit.*

sedēs, is (F.), *seat, abode.*
sēmestris, is, *six months, half-year.*
semper, *always.*
senātus, ūs (M.), *senate.*
senectūs, ūtis (F.), *old age.*
senesco,[3] ere, *grow old, wane.*
senex, senis (M.), *old man.*
sēni, ae, a, *six* (each, at a time), (often in Eng. by the cardinal number).
senīlis, e, *of an old man, characteristic of an old man.*
sententia, ae (F.), *opinion.*
sentio,[4] īre, sēnsi, sēnsum, *feel, notice.*
sepelio,[4] īre, ii, sepultum, *bury.*
septem, *seven.*
sepulcrum, i (N.), *tomb.*
sequor,[3] sequi, secūtus, *follow, ensue.*
sero,[3] ere, serui, sertum, *weave.*
sero,[3] ere, sēvi, satum, *plant, sow.*
serpēns, tis (M.), *serpent.*
servīlis, e, *of slaves.*
servo,[1] āre, āvi, ātum, *serve, keep.*
servus, i (M.), *slave.*
sessio, ōnis (F.), *sitting.*
seu, *or;* seu .. seu, *whether .. or, if either.'. or if,* sometimes *to see if either .. or.*
sevērē, *with severity.*
sevērus, a, um, *stern.*
sī, *if.*
sīc, *so, thus.*
sicuti, *just as.*
Sicilia, ae (F.), *Sicily.*
Siciliēnsis, e, *Sicilian.*
Siculus, a, um, *Sicilian.*
sīcut, *as, as also.*
sīdus, eris (N.), *star, constellation.*
significo,[1] āre, āvi, ātum, *make a sign, signify, indicate.*
signum, i (N.), *mark, sign, standard, statue.*
silentium, i (N.), *silence.*
Silānus, i (M.), *Silanus,* a man's name.
silva, ae (F.), *wood, forest.*

similis, e, *like, similar.*
similitūdo, inis (F.), *likeness.*
simul, *at the same time;* simul ac, *as soon as.*
simulācrum, i (N.), *image, imaginary sounds.*
simulo,¹ āre, āvi, ātum, *feign, pretend.*
sine (abl.), *without.*
singulī, ae, a (distributive numeral), *one by one, one* (though plural).
sino,³ ere, sīvi, situm, *leave, let, permit.*
sitio,³ īre, *thirst.*
sitis, is (F.), *thirst.*
situs, ūs (M.), *neglect, dust.*
situs, a, um (part. of sino), *placed;* est situs, *rests, is situated.*
socer, ceri (M.), *father-in-law.*
sōl, sōlis (M.), *the sun.*
soleo,² ēre, solitus, *be accustomed, be wont.*
sōlitūdo, inis (F.), *solitude.*
sollers, tis, *skilful.*
sollertia, ae (F.), *skill.*
sōlum, *only.*
sōlus, a, um (gen. ius), *alone.*
solvo,³ ere, solvi, solūtum, *loosen, settle* (a dispute).
somnium, i (N.), *dream.*
somnus, i (M.), *sleep.*
sonus, i (M.), *sound.*
sopor, ōris (M.), *sleep.*
sordidus, a, um, *dirty, mean.*
sparsus, a, um (part. of spargo), *scattered.*
spatiōsus, a, um, *spacious.*
spatium, i (N.), *space.*
spatiōsus, a, um, *spacious.*
spatium, i (N.), *space.*
speciēs, iēi (F.), *show, appearance.*
spectābilis, e, *of noble aspect.*
spectāculum, i (N.), *spectacle.*
specto,¹ āre, āvi, ātum, *view, behold, look, face.*
spelunca, ae (F.), *cavern.*
spēs, ei (F.), *hope.*
squālor, ōris (M.), *wretched plight, filth, mourning apparel.*

statio, ōnis (F.), *post, station, picket.*
statua, ae (F.), *statue.*
stella, ae (F.), *star.*
sterno,³ ere, strāvi, strātum, *strew, spread a couch.*
stilus, i (M.), *style* (writing implement).
stimulus, i (M.), *goad.*
stirps, is (F.), *shrub, stock, race.*
sto,¹ stāre, steti, statum, *stand, stop*
stomachor,¹ āri, ātus, *be vexed.*
strepitus, ūs (M.), *noise, rattling.*
struo,³ ere, struxi, structum, *build.*
studeo,² ēre, ui, *be earnest for, favor* (dat.), *study, be a student.*
studium, i (N.), *earnestness, fondness* (for) *study.*
suāvis, e, *sweet.*
suāvitās, ātis (F.), *sweetness, sweet taste.*
sub (abl.), *under.*
subigo,³ ere, ēgi, actum, *subdue, break in.*
subitō, *suddenly.*
Suēvi, ōrum (M.), *Suevi,* a German tribe.
Sulla, ae (M.), *Sulla,* a Roman general.
sum, esse, fui, *I am, be.*
summus, a, um (superl. of superus), *highest, greatest, highest part.*
sūmo, ere, sumpsi, sumptum, *take.*
suovetaurīlia, ium (N.; plur.), *a solemn sacrifice of the Romans.*
supero,¹ āre, āvi, ātum, *surpass.*
supplex, icis (adv.), *suppliant.*
supplicium, i (N.), *supplication,* (capital) *punishment.*
suppōno,³ ere, posui, positum, *put beneath* (dative).
suprā (acc.), *above, on the surface of.*
surculus, i (M.), *sapling.*
sus, suis (C.), *swine.*
suspectus, a, um (part. of following), *suspicious.*

suspicio,³ ere, spexi, spectum, look up to or at, suspect.
sustento,¹ āre, āvi, ātum, sustain, keep alive.
sustineo ² [sub, teneo], ēre, ui, tentum, sustain.
suus, a. um, his (her or their), reflexive.
Syracūsae, a, um (F.), Syracuse, a city of Sicily.
Syracūsānus, a, um, Syracusan.

T.

taberna, ae (F.), shop.
tabula, ae (F.), plank, panel (for pictures), picture.
taeda, ae (F.), pine-tree, torch.
tālis, e, such ; tāle, such a thing.
tamen, yet, nevertheless, however.
tamquam, as if.
tandem, at length.
tango,³ ere, tetigi, tactum, touch.
tantum, so much, only ; (with partitive gen.), so many ; tantum abest, it is so far (from being the case).
tantus, a, um, so great.
Tarentum, i (N.), Tarentum, a town of South Italy.
taurus, i (M.), bull.
tectum, i (N.), roof, dwelling.
tecum = cum and te from tu.
tellūs, ūris (F.), earth.
temperātus, a, um (part. of tempero), tempered, temperate.
tempero,¹ āre, āvi, ātum, moderate, control, restrain. [son.
tempestīvē, seasonably, in seatemplum, i (N.), temple.
tempus, oris (N.), time.
tendo,³ dere, tetendi, tentum, hold, strain.
tenebra, ae (F.), darkness, dark recess.
teneo,² ēre, tenui, tentum, hold, possess, have in one's power.
ter, three times.
tergum, i (N.), back ; a tergo, in the rear.

terra, ae (F.), earth, land.
terreo,³ ēre, ui, itum, alarm, terrify.
terror, ōris (M.), alarm, terror (object of alarm).
Tertia, ae (F.), a woman's name.
tertius, a, um, third.
tesca, ōrum (N.), thickets.
testis, is (M.), witness.
tēter, tra, trum, foul, horrible.
theātrum, i (N.), theatre.
Themistoclēs, is, and i (M.), Themistocles, a Grecian statesman.
Thermopylae, ārum (F.), Thermopylae.
tibia, ae (F.), pipe.
timeo,² ēre, timui, fear.
timesco,³ ere, take alarm.
timidus, a, um, fearful, timid.
timor, ōris (M.), fear.
titulus, i (M.), placard.
tollo, ere, sustuli, sublātum, raise, take up, take away.
tot, so many.
tōtus, a, um, whole, entire ; often with the force of an adverb, wholly.
tragoedia, ae (F.), tragedy.
trāns (acc.), across, beyond.
trānsfuga, ae (M.), deserter.
trecenti, ae, a, three hundred.
tremo,³ ere, tremui, tremble.
tremulus, a, um, trembling.
trepidus, a, um, timid.
tribūnālis, e, of a tribune.
tribūnus, i (M.), tribune.
triennium, i (N.), (space of) three years.
trigintā (indec.), thirty.
triquetra, ae, three-cornered.
tristiculus, a, um, a little sad.
tristis, e, sad, cruel.
trīticum, i (N.), wheat.
Trōja, ae (F.), Troy.
tū, tui, tibi, te, thou (Gr. p. 44).
Tullius, i, name of Cicero.
Tullus, i (M.), a Roman king.
tum, then ; tum . . tum, now . . now.
turpis, e, ugly ; disgraceful, evil.

Vocabulary: Latin and English.

tūs, tūris (N.), *incense.*
tūtus, a, um (part. of tueor), *safe.*
tuus, a, um, *thy, thine, your* (almost always).
Tycha, ae (F.), *name of a city.*
tyrannus, i (M.), *tyrant.*
Tyndaris, idis (F.), *daughter of Tyndarus.*

U.

ūber, era, erum, *rich, fertile.*
ubi, *where, when, where? when?* (interrogative).
ubīque, *everywhere.*
ullus, a, um (gen. ius), *any.*
umbilīcus, i (M.), *navel, centre.*
umquam, *ever* (with negatives and conditions).
unguentum, i (N.), *ointment.*
ūniversus, a, um, *all together.*
unquam, see umquam.
ūnus, a, um (gen. ius), *one.*
urbs, urbis (F.), *city.*
usquam, *anywhere.*
usque, *even, up to.*
ūsus, ūs (M.), *use, advantage, experience.*
ut (with subj.), *that, so that;* (with indic.), *when, as, how, as if.*
uterque, utraque, utrumque (gen. utriusque), *both* (changing the verb to the plural).
uti (ut), *that, so that.*
ūtilis, e, *useful, advantageous.*
ūtilitās, ātis (F.), *utility, advantage, usefulness.*
ūtor,³ ūti, ūsus, *use, employ.*

V.

vacuus, a, um, *empty, unoccupied.*
valdē, *strongly, very, quite.*
valeo,² ēre, valui, *be strong, be well, be worth.*
validus, a, um, *strong* (in almost all senses).
vānus, a, um, *empty, idle, vain.*

varietās, ātis (F.), *variety, variation.*
varius, a, um, *various.*
vastitās, ātis (F.), *devastation.*
vastus, a, um, *vast, waste, desolate.*
vel, *or, even;* vel .. vel, *either .. or.*
velut, *as.*
vēnālis, e, *for sale.* [*sale, sell.*
vendo,³ dere, didi, ditum, *put to*
venio,⁴ īre, vēni, ventum, *come.*
vēnor¹, āri, ātus, *hunt.*
venustās, ātis (F.), *grace, elegance, polish.*
vērē, *truly, with truth, rightly.*
vereor,² ēri, itus, *respect, fear.*
vēritās, ātis (F.), *truth.*
vērō, *in truth, in fact, but, and* (with an emphasis on the word which precedes).
vērus, a, um, *true.*
versus, ūs (M.), *verse.* [*vertex.*
vertex, icis (M.), *head, top,*
vescor,³ vesci (with abl.), *feed upon.*
vesper, eri (M.), *evening;* ad vesperum, *at evening.*
vespera, ae (F.), *evening.*
vestīgium, i (N.), *foot-print, trace.*
vestio,⁴ īre, īvi, ītum, *clothe, cover.*
vestis, is (F.), *clothing, raiment.*
vestītus, ūs (M.), *clothing, garb, covering* (as by woods or the like).
veto,¹ āre, vetui, vetitum, *forbid.*
vetus, eris, *old, ancient.*
vetustās, ātis (F.), *antiquity.*
via, ae (F.), *way, road, course.*
vīcīnum, i (N. of the following), *neighborhood.*
vīcīnus, a, um, *neighboring;* (noun) *neighbor.*
victor, ōris (M.), *conqueror;* (as adj.), *victorious.*
victōria, ae (F.), *victory.*
video,² ēre, vīdi, vīsum, *see.*
videor² (passive), ēri, vīsus, *be seen, seem.* [ne.
videsne = vides, with enclitic

vigil, ilis, *watchful, watchman.*
vigilantia, ae (F.), *watchfulness.*
vigilia, ae (F.), *watching, watch* (the divisions of the Roman night).
vigilo,[1] āre, āvi, ātum, *watch, wake, pass* (a time) *in wakefulness.*
viginti (indec.), *twenty.*
vilis, e, *cheap.*
vilitās, ātis (F.), *cheapness.*
villa, ae (F.), *farm-house, villa.*
villus, i (M.), *shaggy hair* (of animals), *wool.*
vincio,[4] īre, vinxi, vinctum, *bind.*
vinco,[3] ere, vici, victum, *conquer.*
vinculum, i (N.), *bond, tie, chain.*
vindico,[1] āre, āvi, ātum, *assert, claim, punish.*
vir, viri (M.), *man.*
virēs, ium (vis), (F.), *strength.*
virgo, inis (F.), *maiden, virgin.*
virgultum, i (N.), *shrubbery.*
virtūs, ūtis (F.), *manliness, valor, excellence, virtue.*
vis, vis, vim, vi (F.), *force, violence;* (plur.), *energy, strength, power.*

visne = vis (from volo) and enclitic ne.
viscera, um (N.), *flesh.*
vita, ae (F.), *life.*
vitis, is (F.), *grape-vine.*
vitupero,[1] āre, āvi, ātum, *blame, censure.*
vivo,[3] ere, vixi, victum, *live.*
vivus, a, um, *alive, living.*
vix, *with difficulty, scarcely.*
voco,[1] āre, āvi, ātum, *call* (in all senses).
volcānus, i (M.), *fire* (Vulcan).
volo,[1] āre, āvi, ātum, *fly.*
volo, velle, volui (Gr. p. 79), *wish.*
voluntās, ātis (F.), *will, wish, feeling.*
voluptās, ātis (F.), *pleasure.*
vōs, vestrum (i), vōbis, *you* (Gr. p. 44).
vōsmet, *yourselves* (emphatic; see met).
voveo,[2] ēre, vōvi, vōtum, *vow.*
vōx, vōcis (F.), *voice.*
vulgus, i (N.), *the lower classes.*
vulnus, eris (N.), *wound.*
vultus, ūs (M.), *expression, countenance, face.*

INDEX

TO THE SYNTAX OF ALLEN AND GREENOUGH'S LATIN GRAMMAR, WITH PARALLEL REFERENCES TO GILDERSLEEVE'S GRAMMAR.

A. & G.		G.	A. & G.		G.	A. & G.		G.
45	1	192	48	3		50	c	376
	2	,,		a	617		R	,, R
	3	284, 326		b	618, 622		d	381, 382
	4			c	622		e	389 R 2
	5	474		d	618			405 R 3
	6	475, 612		e	616 R 2		R	418 end
	7	201, 202 R 1		4	612 R 1	51		343
	8			5	613 R 1		N	,, R 1
46		202, 319	49		202		1	344
	1	318		R	319 R 1		a	,,
	2	197, 324		1	281 & R 2		b	,, R 1
	a	319		a	283		c	348
	b	412 R 2		b	,, R 2		2	345
	c	319 R 2		c	202 R 1		a	,,
	N	359		d	281 Exc. 1		R	,, R 1
47		202, 285		2	194		R 2	347
	R	324		a	198		R 3	,,
	1	281		b	199 R 3		b	345
	2	286		c	688, 200		c	346, 344
	a	281 Exc. 2	50		357		d	,,
	b	282			360		R 1	330
	c	,,		1	,, R 1		R 2	
	d	202 R 1		a	,, R 3		e	346
	e	202 R 5		b	365			344 R 2
		616 R 3		c	,, R 1		R	,,
	f	202 R 2		d	,, R 2, 3		f	208
	3	195 R 1		e	367 R			345 R 3
	N	,,		f	359		g	344 R 3
	a			g	364			388 R 1
	b	293 R 2		h	,, R		3	349
	c	284 R		i	379		R	,, R 2
		440		R	372		a	346
	4			2	366		b	322
	a	195 R 2		a	369		4	206
	b	,,		b	368		a	353
	c	202 R 4		c	371		b	352
	d	423		R	,, R 2		c	,, R
		535		d	371		R	
	N	195 R 4		e	,, R 7		5	350
	5	360 R 1		R 1	,, R 5		R	,,
	a	,,		R 2	370 R 2		6	356 & R 6
	b	363		R 3	368 R 3		a	,, R 3
	c	,, R 1		R 4	361 R 2		b	,, R 2
	6	324 R 6		3	361		c	,, R 1
	7	314		a	357 R 1		d	,, ,,
	a	,,		b	373, 374		e	,, R 4
	8	287 R		c	374 R 2			355
	9	306		R	,, R 3		7	343
48		616		d	356 R 1		N	,,
	N			R	361 R 1		a	,, R 2
	1	616		4			b	354
	2	,, R 3		a	375		c	,, R
	a	619		R	,, R 1, 2		d	351
	b	618 R 3		b	377 & R 1	52	R	344 R 1
				R	,, R 2			327

Parallel References.

A. & G.	G.	A. & G.	G.	A. & G.	G.
52 R	207	**54** b	401 & R	**57** N	254 R 1
1 N	329	8	404	c	,, R 2
1 N a	207	a	379	5	257, 608, 610
a	329 R 1	R b	380	6	251, 258
b	331		379	7	259
c	329 R 1	9	397	a	264, 266
d	130	10	387	b	267
e	696	a	407, 373 R 1	R	262
f			403 R 3	c	,,
2	333	b	403–9	c R	260 R
a	334	N	408 R	d	265, 268
b	330 R 1	c	438 R 2	8	420
c	333	d	384, 392	N	341 R
c R	,, R 2	**55** 1	392, 337	a	423, 535
d	,, & R 2	a	,, ,,	b	535
3	331 R 2	b	392 R 2	c	424
a	,, ,,	2	335	d	,, R 2, 3
b	,, ,,	N	328	N	271, 4
c	332	a	364 R	e	527
c R	,, R 2	b	335	N	276
4		3	342, 384, 388	R 1	535 R 2
a	340	N	413	R 2	197 R 1
b	527	a	411		527 R 3
c	335–8	b	410	f	341 R
53	194 R 3	R	436		424 R 4
a	,,	c	412	R	,,
b	324 R 1	R	39 R	R	341
54	338	d	412 R 1	R N	534, 560 R
N	,,	e	,, R 3	h	650
1	388–9	f	385–6, 384 R 2	**58**	213
a	388	R	410 R 3, 4	1	270
b	,,		411 R 1	2	218
c	,,	4	387	a	221
d	390	**56**	413	b	218 R 2
R	,,	1	,,	c	219
R e	389 R 2	a	417	d	220
R	373 R 6	b	418	e	,, R 1
2	394	c	419	f	511 R 1
a	395	R	384 R 1	3	222
R	,,	d	419	a	,,
b		e		b	225
c	396 & R 2	f	Appendix	c	224
d	,, R 1	g	418	d	,, R 3
3	406–7	R	,, end	e	246 R 2
N	383	2	416 R	4	234
a	398 R 2	a	App'x; 356 R 4	5	226
b	407 R 1	b	418 R	a	228
c	372 & R	c	417 R	b	569
4	403	d	416 R	c	228 R 2
a	205 R 1	3	566, 576	d	224
b	403	4	403	R	227 R 2
5	399	R	,,	6	233
N	397	5	414 R	7	236
a	311 R 1	**57** 1	245 R	R	,, R 2–4
R	,, R 2	2	246	8	244
b	399 R 2	a	247	9	271
c	311 R 4		250–258	10	510, 216
N	399 R 1		597–599	a	511 R 2
6	401, 403	b	507, 469, 562	b	510 R
a	391, 401, 403	N		c	513
R	346 R 2, 348	3	256	R	,,
b		N	266 R 2	d	
c	389 & R 1	a	266–7	e	511 R 1
R	373 R 6	b	266 R 2	f	599 R 5
d	405	c	575	g	517 R 2
e	400	d	266 R 3	h	519 & R
R		4	253, 255	11	276
7	402	a	253	a	246
a	,, R 1	b	254		

Parallel References.

A. & G.	G.	A. & G.	G.	A. & G.	G.
58 b	277 & R	62 N	582	68 1	253-4
c	530	R 1	"	R 2	254 R 2
d	274	R 2	581 R	2	256
R	275	R 3	582		266
e	"	c	579, 574 R		264
f	246	R	577-9		546 R 1
59	590	d	574-5	3	655
1	"	e	587 & R	69 1	626
a	591 & R 3	N	"	5	
N	628	f	589	(1)	628
b	590	63	538	(2)	
2	596*	1	539, 587 R	a	632
a	"	2	541	b	633
b	568-9	a	636	c	634
N	596*	b	587	d	636, 637
c	596	64 1	544	e	582
3	597	R	545	(3	
a	"	N	"	a	509
b	599	a	545, 2	b	"
N	"	b	688 R	70	507
c	" R 1	R	484 R 2	R 1	526
d	" R 2	c	546		507
e	246 R 3	2	544 R 1 & 2	2	527, 532
f	599 R 3, 5	65 1	553, 554	a	528
4	597-8	R	543, 558 R 4	b	" R
a	597	a	547, 549	c	652 R 2
b	598	b	550, 551	d	527 R 3
c	236 R 2	2	633	3	546
d	597-8	N	"	a	" & R 1
e	195 R 6	a	634	b	532
f	598 R 1	b	633	c	"
5	596*	c	313	R	608
a	597 R 3	d	629 R	d	424
b	599 R 2	e	637		546 & R 2
c	246 R 4	66 1	556 R 2		300
60	594	a	509, 3, 4	e	547, 549
1	"	b	509, 2	f	552
a	"	c	509, 3	R	546 R 3
b	600	d	"		547 R 2
c	"	R	541	E	532 R 4
2	602	N	539 R	4	557
R	613 R 2	2	541 R 1	a	558
a	602	N	"	b	647 R 4
b	252 R 1	67	666	e	560
c	246 R 1-3	1	665	R	" R
R	"	a	651	d	558 R 1
d			" R 1	e	557
61	604 foll.		653	f	559
1	604	a	424 R 3	E	551, 1
R 2	"	R	527 R 2	R	" 2
2	606 foll.	b	644		546 R 2
3	575	R	630 R 1, 2	N	"
4	592	c	638, 644	5	525
a	592 R 2, 5	N	659	a	" R 2
b	" R 4	d	" R 2	b	542, 533
c	597 R 4	R 2	654 R 1	R	
	499	R	469, 654	71	451 foll.
d	606-10	R a	454	1	456-8
62	612 R 2	b	514, 515 R 3	R	455
	561		654 R 2	a	462
1	563	R	470	b	469
	568-9	R	469 R 3	R	454
2	522, 2	d	" R 1	c	460
N	582 R 1, 633	N	"	d	459 R
a	563	e	" R 2	2	460
R 1	564-5	f	462, 603	R	461
R 2	563 R	3	655	a	460
b	582		664	b	459
				c	461 R

Parallel References.

A. & G.		G.	A. & G.		G.	A. & G.		G.
71	d	460, 468	72	b	390	73	3	428
	3	473		b	230		R	,, R 3
	a	,,		c	537		N	427 R 1
	b				comp. 275, 2		3	429 fcll.
72	1	278		d	536, 524 R 1		a	429 & R
	a	,, 373 R		4	279		R	
	b	278 R		a	239, 673		b	430 & R
	c	572 R, 586		b	509 R 3		c	433
	2	438		5	243		d	432, 434
	a	439		a	439		R	
	b	,, R		b	243		N	
	c	243		R	,, R	74		435
	d	,, R			428 R 3		1	436
	3	667		c	431		R	,, R 1
	R	,, R 1	73	1	427		2	437
	a	,, R 2		R	,, R 1, 426		R	,, R 1

SUPPLEMENT.

OUTLINE OF SYNTAX.

I. SUBJECT AND PREDICATE.

46. NOUNS. — A Noun used to describe another, and meaning the same thing, agrees with it in *Case* (p. 103).

1. When in the same part of the sentence (subject or predicate), it is called an *appositive*, and the use is called *apposition*.

2. When used to form a predicate, with a copulative verb, it is called *predicate nominative* (or other case, as it may be).

a. Agreement in *gender* and *number*; *b.* with *locative*; *c.* genitive in agreement with *possessives*.

47. ADJECTIVES agree with their nouns in *gender, number,* and *case* (p. 105).

1. With two or more nouns the adjective is plural.

2. When nouns are of different genders, an attributive adjective agrees with the *nearest*.

a. Of predicate adjectives; *b.* masculine or neuter; *c.* abstracts with neuter adjectives; *d.* agreement by *synesis*; *e.* with appositive or predicate; *f.* with partitive genitive.

3. Adjectives are often used as nouns, the masculines to denote men, and the feminine women (chiefly plural).

a. Possessives; *b.* Demonstratives; *c.* Nouns as adjectives.

4. A neuter adjective may be used as a noun : —

a. Use in the *singular*; *b.* in the *plural*; *c.* as appositive or predicate ; *d.* in agreement with a clause or infinitive.

5. Adjectives denoting *source* or *possession* may be used for the genitive.

a. For genitive of personal pronouns; *b.* genitive in apposition; *c.* for objective genitive (rarely).

6. An adjective is often used to qualify an *act*, having the force of an Adverb.

7. When two qualities are compared, both adjectives are in the comparative, connected by **quam.**

a. Not with **magis;** *b.* Positives with **quam.**

8. Superlatives denoting order and succession often designate *what part* of an object is meant (so **medius, ceterus,** &c.).

9. Alius ... alius, &c., may be used *reciprocally*, or may imply a change of *predicate* as well as of *subject*.

48. RELATIVES.— A Relative agrees with its antecedent in gender and number; but its case depends on the construction of the clause in which it stands (p. 109).

   1. A verb takes the person of the antecedent.
   2. A relative generally agrees in gender with the *appositive*.
    a. Agreement in case by *attraction*; *b.* with implied antecedent.
   3. The antecedent noun sometimes appears in both clauses; usually only in the former; sometimes it is wholly omitted.
    a. When repeated; *b.* a relative clause (*is* or *hic*, antecedent; R., order of clauses); *c.* antecedent omitted; *d.* predicate adjective (superlatives); *e.* *id quod* or *quae res*.
   4. A relative often stands at the beginning of a clause or sentence, where in English a demonstrative must be used.
   5. An Adverb is often equivalent to the pronoun (relative or demonstrative) with a preposition.

49. VERBS.— A verb agrees with its subject-nominative in number and person (p. 112).

   1. Two or more singular subjects take a verb in the plural.
    a. Rule for persons; *b.* with disjunctives; *c.* collective nouns, &c.; *d.* action belonging to the subjects separately.
   2. The subject of a finite verb is in the nominative.
    a. Omission of personal pronoun; *b.* of indefinite subject; *c.* of verb in certain phrases (especially of the *copula*).

II. CONSTRUCTION OF CASES.

50. GENITIVE.— A noun used to limit or define another, and not meaning the same thing, is put in the genitive (p. 113).

   1. **Subjective.** The Genitive is used to denote the author, owner, source, and (with an adjective) measure or quality.
    a. Use of possessives; *b.* omission of limited noun; *c.* genitive in predicate; *d.* with phrase or clause (instead of neuter nominative); so neuter of possessives; *e.* of substance; *f.* instead of appositive; *g.* of quality (with adjectives); *h.* of measure (with numerals); *i.* of quantity, to express value; *k.* with *causa*, &c.
   2. **Partitive.** Words denoting a part are followed by the genitive of the whole to which the part belongs.
    a. Nouns or pronouns; *b.* Numerals, &c.; *c.* Neuter adjectives; *d.* Adverbs; *e* Poetic use.— REMARK 1. Ablative with preposition; 2. uterque; 3. Words meaning a whole; 4. Doubled genitive.
   3. **Objective.** With many nouns and adjectives implying action, the genitive is used to denote the object.
    a. Nouns of action, agency, and feeling; *b.* Adjectives requiring an object of reference (1. desire, &c., 2. verbals, 3. participials);

OUTLINE OF SYNTAX. 239

c. Adjectives with genitive of specification; *d.* of likeness. Use of prepositions in connecting nouns.

4. After Verbs. The genitive is used as the object of several classes of Verbs:—

a. Of *remembering, forgetting,* and *reminding;* *b.* of *accusing, condemning,* and *acquitting;* (peculiar genitives; abl. with de); *c.* of *emotion* (1. pity, &c., 2. impersonals; use of infinitive); *d.* refert and interest; *e.* of *plenty* and *want* (**potior**); *r.* Genitive with Adverbs.

51. DATIVE.—The Dative is used of the object indirectly affected by the action of a verb (p. 121).

1. Of Indirect Object: *with Transitives.* Transitive verbs, whose meaning permits it, take the dative of the indirect object, with the accusative of the direct (as of *giving, telling, sending*).

a. With passive; *b.* Motion with Prepositions; *d.* dono, &c.

2. ———— *after Intransitives.* Intransitive verbs take the dative of the indirect object only.

a. Verbs meaning to *favor, help, please, serve, trust,* and their contraries; also to *believe, persuade, command, obey, envy, threaten, resist, pardon,* and *spare;* (1. **juvo**, &c., with accus.; 2. dat. or acc. with **adulor**, &c.; 3. dat. or acc. according to their meaning); *b.* **libet**, &c.; *c.* with accus. of remote; *d.* Compounds with **ad, ante, con,** &c. (transitive compounds; **obvius**); *e.* Compounds with **ab, de, ex**; *f.* Impersonal use in the passive; *g.* Poetic use of dative.

3. Of Possession. The Dative is used with **esse** and similar words to denote the *Owner.*

REM.—Use of **habeo**; *a.* Compounds of **esse**; *b.* **nomen est.**

4. Of Agency. The Dative is used after some passive forms to denote the *Agent.*

a. Gerund or gerundive; *b.* perfect participle; *c.* poetic use.

5. Of Service. The Dative is used to denote the purpose or end; often with another dative of the person or thing affected.

6. Of Nearness. The Dative is used after words of fitness, nearness, likeness, service, inclination, and their opposites.

a. Accusative with **ad**; *b.* Accusative with **in** or **erga**; *c.* possessive genitive; *d.* **propior**, &c. with acc.; *e.* dat. with verbals.

7. Of Reference. The Dative is often required not by any particular word, but by the general meaning of the sentence.

a. Instead of possessive genitive; *b.* relations of direction; *c.* of volens, nolens; *d.* Ethical Dative (ablative with **pro**).

52. ACCUSATIVE.—The Accusative denotes that which is immediately affected by the action of the verb.

1. The Accusative is the case of the Direct Object.

a. With verbs of feeling; *b.* Cognate Accusative; *c.* with verbs of sensation; *d.* of motion (compounds); *e.* Constructio prægnans; *f.* Impersonals, decet, &c.

2. Two Accusatives. Several verbs take a second accusative, either in apposition or as a secondary object.

a. Verbs of naming, choosing, &c.; *b.* Compounds with prepositions; *c.* Verbs of asking and teaching (passive use); *d.* celo, lateo.

3. Adverbial Accusative. The accusative is used adverbially, or for specification.

b. Accusative of neuter pronoun or adjective; *b.* Adverbial phrases; *c.* Greek accusative: passive used reflexively.

4. Special Uses:—

a. Exclamations; *b.* as subject of Infinitive; *c.* Duration of Time and extent of Space.

53. VOCATIVE. — The Vocative is the form of direct Address (p. 134).

a. Nominative with Imperative; *b.* Vocative of adjective.

54. ABLATIVE. — The Ablative is used to denote the relations expressed in English by the prepositions *from, in, at, with, by* (p. 134).

1. Separation. Verbs meaning to *remove, set free, be absent, deprive,* and *want,* are followed by the ablative.

a. Compounds, used figuratively; *b.* ablative of place *from*; *c.* adjectives of *freedom* and *want*; *d.* opus and usus; egeo and indigeo with genitive (so other words of separation and want).

2. Source. The ablative is used to denote source or material.

a. Participles of birth and origin; *b.* place of birth; *c.* of material, with constare; *d.* with facere, &c.

3. Cause. The ablative is used to express cause.

a. dignus, indignus, and certain verbs; *b.* motive expressed with ob or propter; *c.* causa, gratia.

4. Agent. The voluntary agent after a passive verb is put in the ablative with ab.

a. So with neuters; *b.* agent as instrument with per or opera.

5. Comparison. The comparative degree is followed by the ablative, signifying *than.*

a. Use of quam; *b.* idiomatic ablatives, opinione, &c.; *c.* construction of plus, amplius, &c.

6. Means. The ablative is used to denote accompaniment, means, instrument.

a. Accompaniment with cum (misceo, jungo); *b.* contention with cum; *c.* with words of *fulness*; *d.* utor, &c.; *e.* abl. of *degree of difference* (eo, quo, &c.).

7. Quality. The ablative is used (with an adjective or limiting genitive) to denote *manner* and *quality.*

a. Physical characteristics; *b.* manner with cum; modo, &c.

8. Price. The price of a thing is put in the ablative.

a. Certain genitives of quantity are used to denote *indefinite value;* *b.* so of certain nouns.

9. Specification. The ablative denotes that in respect to which any thing is or is done, or in accordance with which any thing happens.

10. Locative. The ablative of the place where is retained in many idiomatic expressions.

a. Verbs and Verbals.

b. ABLATIVE ABSOLUTE: *A noun or pronoun, with a participle* [forming the subject and predicate of a subordinate clause] *may be put in the ablative to define the time or circumstances of an action;* *c.* Ablative of neuter adjective; *d.* Ablative of place where and time when.

55. TIME AND PLACE. — 1. Time. Time *when* (or within which) is put in the ablative; time *how long* in the accusative.

a. Use of preposition; *b.* Ablative of duration.

2. Space. Extent of space is put in the accusative.

a. Genitive of measure; *b.* Distance in accusative or ablative.

3. Place. To express relations of place, prepositions are necessary, except with the names of towns and small islands.

a. The name of the place *from which* is in the ablative.

b. The name of the place *to which* is in the accusative (so certain phrases; also the former supine).

c. The name of the place *where* takes the locative form, which in the 1st and 2d declensions singular is the same as the *genitive;* in the plural and in the 3d declension, the same as the *dative* (or ablative).

d. **domi, belli, militiæ, humi, ruri,** &c.; *e.* possessives with **domus;** *f.* special phrases.

4. Way. The way *by which* is put in the ablative.

56. PREPOSITIONS. — 1. Prepositions govern the accusative or ablative (p. 146).

a. Those governing accus.; *b.* those governing abl.; *c.* **in, sub** (**pono, statuo,** &c.); *d.* **super;** *e.* **subter;** *f.* Dates; *g.* **tenus.**

2. Many words may be construed either as prepositions or as adverbs.

a. **pridie, propius,** &c., with accus.; *b.* **palam,** &c., with abl.; *c.* **clam;** *d.* Prepos. as adverbs (**ante,** &c).

3. Prepositions or adverbs implying comparison are followed by **quam.**

4. The ablative with **a** or **ab** is regularly used after passive verbs to denote the agent (if a person).

5. Many prepositions sometimes follow their nouns.

III. SYNTAX OF THE VERB.

57. Moods. — The Moods of a Latin verb are the Indicative, Subjunctive, Imperative, and Infinitive (p. 148).

1. INDICATIVE. The Indicative is the mood of direct assertions or questions.

2. SUBJUNCTIVE. The Subjunctive is used in special constructions, both in dependent and independent clauses.

a. INDEPENDENT: hortatory, optative, concessive, dubitative; also in apodosis; *b.* DEPENDENT: purpose or result, temporal clauses, indirect discourse, intermediate clauses.

3. **Hortatory.** The Subjunctive is used (present or perfect) to express a command or exhortation.

a. Second person of indefinite subj.; *b.* perfect in prohibitions; *c.* proviso; *d.* past obligation.

4. **Optative.** The subj. is used to denote a wish: primary tenses when conceived as possible; secondary, as unaccomplished.

a. Old use of perfect; *b.* ut, utinam, O si; velim, vellem.

5. **Concessive**: the subjunctive is used to express a concession (with or without ut, quamvis, quamlibet, &c.).

6. **Dubitative**: the subjunctive is used in questions implying doubt, indignation, or an impossibility of the thing being done.

7. IMPERATIVE. The Imperative is used in *commands;* also, by early writers and poets, in *prohibitions.*

a. Prohibitions (perf. subj., noli, cave, fac ne); *b.* use of pres. subj.; *c.* future imperative; *d.* future for imperative.

8. INFINITIVE. The Infinitive denotes the action of the verb as an abstract noun.

a. As subject or object (esse and impersonals); *b.* with impersonals as subj. or complement; *c.* Complementary Infinitive; *d.* used optionally; *e.* with subj.-accus., after words of *knowing, thinking,* and *telling; f.* Purpose; *g.* Exclamations; *h.* Historical Infinitive.

58. TENSES. — The Tenses are the Present, Imperfect, Future of incomplete action, and the Perfect, Pluperfect, and Future Perfect of completed action (p. 157).

1. The tenses of the INDICATIVE denote *absolute time.*

2. **Present.** The Present denotes an action or state as now existing, as incomplete, or as indefinite.

a. Action continuing; *b.* Conative Present; *c.* Present for future; *d.* Historical Present; *e.* with dum; *f.* of extant writers.

3. **Imperfect.** The imperfect denotes an action or condition continued or repeated in past time.

a. Descriptions; *b.* action continuing; *c.* conative; *d.* surprise; *e.* in narrative (comic).

4. Future. The Future denotes an action or condition that will occur hereafter.

5. Perfect. The perfect *definite* denotes an action as now completed; the perfect *historical*, as having taken place indefinitely in past time.

a. As no longer existing; *b.* of indefinite time; *c.* of general truth (*gnomic*), especially negations; *d.* in negations preferred to imperfect.

6. Pluperfect. The Pluperfect is used to denote an action completed in time past; sometimes also repeated in indefinite time.

7. Future Perfect. The Future Perfect denotes an action as completed in the future.

8. Epistolary Tenses. In Letters, the perfect or imperfect may be used for the present, and the pluperfect for past tenses.

9. SUBJUNCTIVE. In Independent clauses, the Present Subjunctive always refers to *future* time, the Imperfect to either *past* or *present*; the Perfect to either *future* or *past*; the Pluperfect always to *past*.

In Dependent clauses, the tenses of the subjunctive denote *relative time*, not with reference to the speaker, but to the action of some other verb.

10. Sequence of Tenses. In compound sentences, a primary tense in the leading clause is followed by a primary tense in the dependent clause; and a secondary tense is followed by a secondary (p. 162).

a. Perfect definite; *b.* Perfect subjunctive; *c.* Perfect in clauses of *result* (compared with imperf.); *d.* general truths; *e.* historical present; *f.* Protasis and Apodosis; *g.* imperfect subjunctive in leading clauses; *h.* secondary tenses by *synesis*.

11. INFINITIVE. The tenses of the Infinitive are present, past, or future relatively to the time of the verb on which they depend.

a. Present, following verb in past tense; *b.* Perfect (**memini**); *c.* Present, without reference to time; *d.* Perf. with verbs of *wishing*, &c.; *e.* Perf. with verbs of feeling (poetic); *f.* Future (**fore ut**).

59. CONDITIONAL SENTENCES. — A conditional sentence (or clause) is one beginning with IF or some equivalent.

1. Protasis and Apodosis. The clause containing the *condition* (IF) is called the Protasis; that containing the conclusion is called the Apodosis.

a. Protasis: IF or indef. relative; *b.* Apodosis the main clause.

2. Particular and General Conditions: —

a. A particular supposition refers to a definite act (or series of acts) occurring at some definite time.

b. A general supposition refers to any one of a class of acts which may occur (or may have occurred) at any time.

c. Classification of conditional sentences (p. 167).

3. Present and Past Conditions.—

a. In the statement of a condition whose falsity is not implied, the tenses of the Indicative are used.

b. In the statement of a supposition known to be false, the imperfect and pluperfect subjunctive are used.

c. Imperf. subj. referring to past; *d.* Indic. in apodosis; *e.* expressions of necessity, duty, &c.; *f.* Fut. part. with fui = plup. subj.

4. Future Conditions:—

a. Use of future indic.; *b.* of present. subj.; *c.* of future perf. *d.* Form of Apodosis; *e.* Perfect indic. in apodosis; *f.* Imperf. (or pluperf.) subj. by sequence of tenses.

5. General Conditions:—

a. Indefinite subject (2d person singular); *b.* repeated action (imperfect subj. and indic.); *c.* in other cases, indicative.

60. IMPLIED CONDITIONS. — In many sentences, the condition is stated in some other form than a conditional clause, or is implied in the nature of the thought (p. 172).

1. Condition Disguised:—

a. In a relative or participial clause; *b.* in a wish or command; *c.* in an independent clause.

2. Condition Omitted:—

a. Potential Subjunctive; *b.* Subjunctive of modesty; *c.* Indicative of necessity, duty, &c.; *d.* mixed constructions.

61. CONDITIONAL PARTICLES. Certain particles implying a condition are followed by the subjunctive (p. 174).

1. Comparative:—tamquam, &c. (with pres. or perf. subj.).

2. Concessive:—quamvis, ut, licet, etsi.

3. Proviso:—modo, dum, dummodo.

4. Use of the Conditional Particles:—

a. si, nisi; *b.* nisi vero (objection); *c.* sive (alternative); *d.* concessive particles.

62. RELATIONS OF TIME. Temporal clauses are introduced by particles which are almost all of relative origin; and are usually construed like other relative clauses (p. 176).

1. Temporal particles are used as indefinite relatives.

2. Temporal clauses of *absolute time* take the Indicative; those of *relative time*, the Subjunctive.

a. postquam, ut, ubi; *b.* cum temporal; *c.* antequam, priusquam; *d.* dum, donec, quoad; *e.* cum causal; *f.* cum ... tum.

63. CAUSE OR REASON. Causal Clauses may take the Indicative or Subjunctive according to their construction (p. 181):—

1. Indicative in direct construction;

2. Subjunctive of indirect discourse.

a. Relative clause of characteristic; *b.* cum causal.

64. PURPOSE. — **1.** Final clauses take the Subjunctive after relatives, or the conjunction ut, -ne (p. 182).

a. Use of quo; *b.* Suppression of principal clause.

2. Purpose is expressed in various ways; but never (except rarely in poetry) by the simple Infinitive (p. 183).

65. CONSEQUENCE OR RESULT. — **1.** Consecutive Clauses take the Subjunctive after relatives or the conj. ut, ut non (p. 183).

a. quominus; *b.* quin (substantive clause).

2. A relative clause of Result is often used to indicate a *characteristic* of the antecedent.

a. General expressions of existence, &c.; *b.* unus and solus; *c.* Comparatives with quam; *d.* restriction or proviso; *e.* cause or hinderance; *f.* dignus, aptus, idoneus.

66. INTERMEDIATE CLAUSES. A subordinate clause takes the Subjunctive when it expresses the thought of some other person than the speaker or writer; or when it is an integral part of a subjunctive clause or an equivalent infinitive (p. 185).

1. The Subjunctive is used in intermediate clauses to express the thought of some other person.

a. Indirect discourse; *b.* depending on implied wish, command, &c.; *c.* main clause merged in a verb of saying; *d.* reason with quod (non quod, non quin).

2. A clause depending on another subjunctive clause (or equivalent infinitive) will also take the subjunctive if regarded *as an integral part of that clause.*

67. INDIRECT DISCOURSE. — A Direct Quotation is one which gives the exact words of the original speaker or writer. An Indirect Quotation is one which adapts the original words to the structure of the sentence in which they are quoted.

1. Indirect Narrative. In a declaratory sentence in indirect discourse, the principal verb is in the Infinitive, and its subject in the Accusative. All subordinate clauses take the Subjunctive.

a. Subject-accusative; *b.* Relative clauses; *c.* Conditional Sentences; *d.* Questions: indirect or rhetorical.

2. Indirect Questions. An indirect question takes its verb in the Subjunctive.

a. Future participle; *b.* Dubitative Subjunctive; *c.* Accusative of anticipation; *d.* Early use of indicative; *e.* Indefinites (nescio quis); *f.* clauses with si (*whether*).

3. Indirect Commands. All imperative forms of speech take the Subjunctive in indirect discourse.

68. WISHES AND COMMANDS. — **1.** Wishes are expressed by the Subjunctive: the primary tenses in reference to future time, the secondary to express a hopeless wish (p. 192).

2. Commands are expressed by the Imperative or Subjunctive; Prohibitions by the subjunctive or a periphrasis with **noli, cave**. The Object of a command is given in a purpose-clause.

3. Indirectly quoted, all these forms take the Subjunctive.

69. RELATIVE CLAUSES. — **1.** A simple relative, merely introducing a descriptive fact, takes the Indicative.

2. In relative clauses with the Subjunctive, the relative is either in protasis, or expresses some logical connection, or has no effect on the construction (as in indirect discourse).

70. SUBSTANTIVE CLAUSES. — A Substantive Clause is one which is the subject or object of a verb, or in apposition with a subject or object (p. 193).

1. Classification: 1. Infinitive Clauses; 2. Indirect Questions; 3. Clauses of *purpose* or *result* (ut); 4. Indicative of *fact* (quod).

2. The Infinitive (with accusative) is used as the Subject chiefly of esse and impersonal verbs; as the Object, 1. of verbs and expressions of *knowing, thinking,* and *telling;* 2. **jubeo, veto,** &c.; 3. of verbs of *wishing.*

a. After passives; *b.* poetic extension; *c.* verb of *saying* implied; *d.* verbs of *promising,* &c.

3. Clauses of Purpose are used as the object of all verbs denoting an *action directed towards the future.*

a. Verbs of *commanding,* &c.; *b.* of *wishing,* &c.; *c.* of *permission,* &c.; *d.* of *determining,* &c. (*decreeing,* with part. in **dus**); *e.* of *caution* and *effort;* *f.* of *fearing* (**ne, ut**); *g.* poetic use of infinitive.

4. Clauses of Result are used as the object of verbs denoting the *accomplishment of an effort.*

a. Verbs of *happening,* &c.; *b.* following **quam**; *c.* in exclamations (elliptically); *d.* **tantum abest**; *e.* **facere ut**; *f.* instead of accus. and infin.; *g.* hindering (**quin**; **non dubito**); *h.* Use optional.

5. The Indicative with **quod** is used (more commonly as subject) when the statement is regarded as a fact.

a. As accus. of specification; *b.* with verbs of *feeling* (**miror si**).

71. QUESTIONS. — Questions are introduced by interrogative pronouns, adverbs, or particles, and are not distinguished by the order of words (p. 200).

1. Interrogative Particles: —

a. **num** in indirect questions; *b.* form of indirect questions; *c.* enclitic **-ne**; *d.* **nescio an**, &c.

2. Double Questions (**utrum ... an**): —

a. Omission of former particle; *b.* of first member; *c.* of second member; *d.* forms of alternative.

3. Question and Answer. In answering a question, the verb is generally repeated.

72. PARTICIPLES. — The Participle expresses the action of the verb in the form of an adjective (p. 202).

1. Distinctions of Tense: —
a. Present; *b.* Perfect (deponent); *c.* Pres. passive (dum, -dus).

2. Adjective Use, attributive: —
a. As nouns; *b.* as predicate with **esse**; *c.* periphrastic perfect; *d.* two forms of perfect passive.

3. Predicate Use. The present and perfect participles are often used to express time, cause, occasion, condition, concession, characteristic, manner, circumstance (especially in the *Ablative Absolute*).

a. Passive part. containing the main idea; *b.* Perfect part. with **habeo**; *c.* with **volo**; Present part. for infin. (with **facio**, &c.).

4. Future Participle: —
a. Periphrastic conjugation; *b.* with fui, &c., for pluperf. subj.

5. Gerundive (denoting necessity and propriety): —
a. in simple agreement; *b.* periphrastic conjugation (impersonal use); *c.* with verbs of *undertaking, demanding*, &c.

73. GERUND AND GERUNDIVE. — **1.** The Gerund, in grammatical construction, follows the same rules as nouns (p. 206).

2. Gerundive. When the Gerund would have an object in the accusative, the Gerundive is generally used instead, agreeing with the noun, in the case which the gerund would have had.

3. Construction. The Gerund and Gerundive are used in the oblique cases in the constructions of nouns: —

a. The Genitive is used as objective genitive after nouns or adjectives, as a predicate with **esse**, or as a genitive of quality.
b. The Dative is used after the adjectives (rarely nouns) which are followed by the dative of nouns; sometimes also after verbs.
c. The Accusative is used after several prepositions; most frequently after **ad** denoting purpose.
d. The Ablative is used to express means, instrument, or manner, after comparatives, and after several prepositions.
e. The Gerund is occasionally found in apposition with a noun.

74. Supine. — **1.** The Former Supine is used after verbs of motion, to express the purpose of the motion (p. 209).

2. The Latter Supine is used only after a few adjectives and nouns, to denote that in respect to which the quality is asserted.

SYNOPSIS OF CONSTRUCTIONS.

[The figures refer to *pages*.]

I. SUBJECT AND PREDICATE.

NOUN: agreement in case
- 1. Apposition
  - of abl. with locative, 104.
  - of gen. with possessive, 105.
- 2. Predicate Agreement, 104.

ADJECTIVE: Attributive, Predicate, Appositive
- Agreement
  - with nearest noun, 105.
  - by *synesis*, 106.
- as Noun
  - masc. or fem., of persons, 106.
  - neut. as object, quality, &c., 107.
- Possessive, as genitive (subj. or obj.), 108.
- as Adverb, qualifying the act, 108.

RELATIVE:
- Agreement
  - with appositive, 110.
  - in case by attraction, 110.
- Antecedent noun
  - in either or both clauses, 110.
  - omitted, 110.

II. CONSTRUCTION OF CASES.

NOMINATIVE: as Subject of a Finite Verb, 112.

GENITIVE:
1. Subjective (source, possession, quality), 114.
2. Partitive (with numerals, superlatives, &c.), 115.
3. Objective
   - with nouns and adjectives of agency, 117.
   - with verbs
     - of memory and feeling, 119, 120.
     - of charge and penalty, 119.

DATIVE:
1. Of Indirect Object
   - with transitives, 121.
   - with intransitives, 122.
2. Of Possession
   - with *ease*, 126.
   - with *nomen est*, 127.
3. Of Agency
   - with gerundive, 127.
   - with other passive forms, 127.
4. Of Service (denoting purpose or end), 128.
5. Of Nearness, fitness, likeness, &c., 128.
6. Of Reference (*dativus commodi*), 129.

ACCUSATIVE:
1. Of Direct Object (including *cognate accusative*), 131.
2. Of Apposition or Secondary object, 132.
3. Adverbial (including accusative of specification), 133.
4. Of Exclamation, 133.
5. As subject of Infinitive, 133.

VOCATIVE: of Direct Address.

ABLATIVE:
- 1. Original Ablative (FROM)
  - of separation and want, 135.
  - of source, 136.
  - of cause, 137.
  - of agent (with *ab*), 138.
  - of comparison (*than*), 138.
- 2. Instrumental (WITH)
  - of means and accompaniment, 139.
  - of quality (with adjectives), 141.
  - of price, 141.
  - of specification, 142.
- 3. Locative (IN, AT)
  - Place *where*, 145.
  - Time *at* or *within which*, 143.
  - Idiomatic use, 142.
  - Circumstance (ABLATIVE ABSOLUTE), 142.

SYNOPSIS OF CONSTRUCTIONS. 249

III. SYNTAX OF THE VERB.

MOODS:
- INDICATIVE: Direct assertion or question; Absolute Time, 148.
- SUBJUNCTIVE:
  - Hortatory, Optative, Concessive, Dubitative, 148.
  - Dependent:
    - Purpose or Result, 181, 183. [177.
    - Characteristic, 184; Relative Time,
    - Indirect Discourse { Subordinate, 188.
      Indir. Quest. 190.
    - Conditions { Future, 170.
      Contrary to fact, 168.
- IMPERATIVE: Commands, Prohibitions, 152.
- INFINITIVE:
  - as Subject or Object; Complementary, 154.
  - of Indirect Discourse (subject-accusative), 188.
  - of Purpose; Exclamation; Historical, 156.

CONDITIONS:
- Expressed
  - Present or Past { simple condition (indic.), 168.
    contrary to fact (subj.), 168.
  - Future { more vivid (fut. indic.), 170.
    less vivid (pres. subj.), 170.
  - General { indef. subject (2d person), 171.
    repeated action, 171.
- Implied
  - Disguised { by qualifying clause, 172.
    by wish, command, &c., 172.
    independent clause, 173.
  - Omitted { potential subjunctive, 173.
    subjunctive of modesty, 173.
    (indic. of necessity, &c., 174.)
    mixed constructions, 174.

INDIRECT DISCOURSE:
- Narration
  - Principal clause: Accus. and Infin., 188.
  - Subordinate clauses, Subj.: { Relative, 188.
    Conditional, 188.
    Imperative, 191.
- Question (Subjunctive) { Interrog. phrase, 190.
  Accus. of anticipation, 190.
  nescio quis, mirum si, 191.
- Intermediate Clauses (Subjunctive), 186.

SUBSTANTIVE CLAUSES:
- Accus. and Infin. (or Infin. alone) { as Subject (esse and impers.), 153.
  as Object { Indir. Discourse, 194.
    Wishes or Commands, 195.
- Subjunctive with UT { Purpose (command, wish, fear), 196.
  Result (happen, effect, hinder), 197.
- Indicative with QUOD: fact, specification, feeling, 199.
- Indirect Questions, 190.

PARTICIPLES:
- Present and Perfect
  - Simple predicate, 203.
  - Periphrastic perfect, 203.
  - Predicate of circumstance, 204.
  - (Ablative Absolute), 204.
  - Present, descriptive (indir. disc.), 205.
- Future { Periphrastic with esse, 205.
  " with fui = pluperf. subj., 169.
- Gerundive { as descriptive adjective, 205.
  periphrastic with esse, 205.
  of purpose, with certain verbs, 206.

GERUND (like Infinitive) and GERUNDIVE (in agreement with noun):
- Genitive: as objective gen., 207.
- Dative: with adjectives, &c., 208.
- Accusative: with prepositions, 208.
- Ablative: { of manner and instrum., 208.
  with prepositions, 208.

SUPINE { Former Supine: with verbs of motion, 209.
Latter Supine: with adjectives, nouns, verbs, 209.

Announcements.

JUST PUBLISHED.

ALLEN & GREENOUGH'S LATIN COURSE.

The **Cicero, Shorter Course, Virgil, Cæsar, De Senectute, Sallust's Catiline,** and **Latin Lessons** refer to ALLEN & GREENOUGH'S and GILDERSLEEVE'S Grammars.

Wholesale. Retail.

THE BUCOLICS OF VIRGIL. With Introduction, Notes, and Grammatical References to Allen & Greenough's and Gildersleeve's Latin Grammars. The text is founded on that of Kibbock, variations from that and from Heyne being given in the Margin.

THE ÆNEID OF VIRGIL. Six Books, making one volume with the Bucolics.

CÆSAR'S GALLIC WAR. Four Books. In the same style with Sallust's Catiline. Grammatical References to Allen & Greenough and to Gildersleeve.

SELECTIONS FROM OVID. (Chiefly from the Metamorphoses.) Uniform in style and general plan with Virgil.

SALLUST'S CATILINE $0.80 $1.00

AN INTRODUCTION TO LOGARITHMS; with an Explanation of the Author's three and four place Tables. By JAMES MILLS PEIRCE, University Professor of Mathematics in Harvard University . . . 1.00

The requisites for admission to *Harvard College* now include "*the use and the rudiments of the theory of Logarithms*"; and "*the examples requiring the use of logarithms at the examination will be adapted to a four-place table.*" The above-named works are suitable to prepare students for this examination.

This book, with the tables by the same author, contains all that is ordinarily taught in schools and colleges on the subject of logarithms, except what is contained in treatises on the Calculus, and *all that is required for admission to Harvard College.*

CICERO DE SENECTUTE (Cato Major), a Dialogue on Old Age. Uniform in style with Allen & Greenough's Cicero, and prepared under the same joint editorship 75

ARNOLD'S MANUAL OF ENGLISH LITERATURE, Historical and Critical. With an Appendix on English Metres. By THOMAS ARNOLD, M. A., of University College, Oxford. Third Edition, revised . . 2 50

HARVARD EXAMINATION PAPERS. Collected and arranged by R. F. LEIGHTON, A. M., Master of Melrose High School . . 1.25 1.56
Second Edition, containing Papers of June and September, 1874.

	Wholesale.	Retail.

OUR WORLD, No. II.; or, Second Series of Lessons in Geography. By MARY L. HALL. With fine illustrations of the various countries, the inhabitants and their occupations, and two distinct series of Maps, 5 pages physical, and 19 pages of finely engraved copperplates political . . $1.60 . . $2.00

This book is intended, if used in connection with the First Lessons, to cover the usual course of geographical study. It is based upon the principle that it is more useful to give vivid conceptions of the physical features and political associations of different regions than to make pupils familiar with long lists of places and a great array of statistics.

PEIRCES TABLES OF LOGARITHMIC and TRIGONOMETRIC FUNCTIONS TO THREE AND FOUR PLACES OF DECIMALS. By JAMES MILLS PEIRCE, University Professor of Mathematics at Harvard University. Cloth . . . . .60 .75

PEIRCE'S ELEMENTS OF LOGARITHMS; with an Explanation of the Author's THREE AND FOUR PLACE TABLES. By JAMES MILLS PEIRCE, University Professor of Mathematics at Harvard University . .80 1.00

This Work is a Companion to THREE AND FOUR PLACE TABLES OF LOGARITHMIC AND TRIGONOMETRIC FUNCTIONS, by the same Author.

STEWART'S ELEMENTARY PHYSICS. American Edition. With QUESTIONS and EXERCISES. By PROF. G. A. HILL, of Harvard University 1.40 1.75

The Questions will be direct and exhaustive upon the text of Mr. Stewart's work. After the Questions will be given a series of easy Exercises and Problems, designed, in the hands of a good teacher, to arouse and strengthen in the student's mind the power of reasoning in accordance with sound scientific methods.

SEARLE'S OUTLINES OF ASTRONOMY. By ARTHUR SEARLE, of Harvard College Observatory.

PRIMARY ARITHMETIC. By G. L. DEMAREST . .40 .50

THE CHANDLER DRAWING-BOOK. By the late JOHN S. WOODMAN, of Dartmouth College 80 1.00

THE NATIONAL MUSIC COURSE. In Four Books. For Public Schools. By JULIUS EICHBERG, J. B. SHARLAND, L. W. MASON, H. E. HOLT, Supervisors of Music in Public Schools of Boston, Mass.

PRIMARY OR FIRST MUSIC READER . . . . . .24 .30
A course of exercises in the elements of VOCAL MUSIC AND SIGHT-SINGING, with choice rote songs for the use of youngest pupils.

INTERMEDIATE MUSIC READER . . . . . . .56 .70
Including the Second and Third Music Readers. A course of instruction in the elements of Vocal Music and Sight-Singing, with choice rote songs, in two and three parts, based on the elements of harmony.

THE FOURTH MUSIC READER. 8vo. pp. 336 . . . . 1.20 1.50
This work, prepared to follow the Third Music Reader, is also adapted, under a competent instructor, to be used in High Schools where no previous systematic instruction has been given. To this end a brief but thorough elementary course is given, with musical theory, original solfeggios, a complete system of triad practice, and sacred music and song, with accompaniment for the piano. The music introduced is of a high order, and by the best masters, and is calculated to cultivate the taste, as well as to extend the knowledge and skill of the pupils.

THE ABRIDGED FOURTH MUSIC READER. 1.00 1.25
SECOND MUSIC READER. . . . . .32 .40
THIRD MUSIC READER . . . . .32 .40

THE NATIONAL MUSIC CHARTS. By LUTHER WHITING MASON. An invaluable aid to Teachers of Common Schools in imparting a practical knowledge of Music, and teaching Children to sing at sight. In Four Series. Forty Charts each Price, $10.00 each Series.
FIRST SERIES, SECOND SERIES, and THIRD SERIES, each 10.00
FOURTH SERIES, by L. W. MASON and J. B. SHARLAND 10.00
EASEL 1.25

THE NATIONAL MUSIC TEACHER. A Practical Guide for Teaching Vocal Music to Young Children. By L. W. MASON . . .60

GREEK.

Wholesale. Retail.

GOODWIN'S GREEK GRAMMAR. By WILLIAM W. GOODWIN, Ph. D., Eliot Professor of Greek Literature in Harvard University. Half morocco $1.25 $1.50

The object of this Grammar is to state *general principles* clearly and distinctly, with special regard to those who are preparing for college. In the sections on the Moods are stated, for the first time in an elementary form, the principles which are elaborated in detail in the author's "Syntax of the Greek Moods and Tenses."

GREEK MOODS AND TENSES. The Fourth Edition. By WILLIAM W. GOODWIN, Eliot Professor of Greek Literature in Harvard University. 1 vol. 12mo. Cloth. pp. 264 . . . . 1.40 1.75

This work was first published in 1860, and it appeared in a new form — much enlarged and in great part rewritten — in 1865. In the present edition the whole has been again revised; some sections and notes have been rewritten, and a few notes have been added. The object of the work is to give a plain statement of the principles which govern the construction of the Greek Moods and Tenses, — the most important and the most difficult part of Greek Syntax.

GOODWIN'S GREEK READER. Consisting of Extracts from Xenophon, Plato, Herodotus, and Thucydides; being a full equivalent for the seven books of the Anabasis, now required for admission at Harvard. With Maps, Notes, References to GOODWIN'S GREEK GRAMMAR, and parallel References to CROSBY'S and HADLEY'S GRAMMARS. Edited by PROFESSOR W. W. GOODWIN, of Harvard College, and J. H. ALLEN, Cambridge. Half morocco 1.60 2.00

This book contains the third and fourth books of the Anabasis (entire), the greater part of the second book of the Hellenica, and the first chapter of the Memorabilia, of Xenophon; the last part of the Apology, and the beginning and end of the Phaedo, of Plato; selections from the sixth, seventh, and eighth books of Herodotus, and from the fourth book of Thucydides.

LEIGHTON'S GREEK LESSONS. Prepared to accompany Goodwin's Greek Grammar. By R. F. LEIGHTON, Master of Melrose High School. Half morocco 1.25 1.56

This work contains about one hundred lessons, with a progressive series of exercises (both Greek and English), mainly selected from the first book of Xenophon's Anabasis. The exercises on the Moods are sufficient, it is believed, to develop the general principles as stated in the Grammar. The text of four chapters of the Anabasis is given entire, with notes and references. Full vocabularies accompany the book.

These lessons, with the additional exercises to be translated into Greek, are believed to be a sufficient preparation in Greek Composition for admission to any American College.

LIDDELL & SCOTT'S GREEK-ENGLISH LEXICON. Abridged from the new Oxford Edition. 13th Edition.
Morocco back 2 40 3.00
Sheep binding 2 80 3.50

LIDDELL & SCOTT'S GREEK-ENGLISH LEXICON. The sixth Oxford Edition unabridged. 4to. Morocco back . 9.60 12.00
Sheep binding . 10.40 13.00

We have made arrangements with Messrs. Macmillan & Co. to publish in this country their new edition of Liddell & Scott's Greek Lexicons, and are ready to supply the trade.

The English editions of Liddell & Scott are *not stereotyped*; but each has been thoroughly revised, enlarged, and printed anew. The sixth edition, just published, is larger by one eighth than the fifth, and contains 1865 pages. It is an *entirely different* work from the first edition, the whole department of etymology having been rewritten in the light of modern investigations, and the forms of the irregular verbs being given in greater detail by the aid of Veitch's Catalogue. No student of Greek can afford to dispense with this invaluable Lexicon, the price of which is now for the first time brought within the means of the great body of American scholars.

THE ŒDIPUS TYRANNUS OF SOPHOCLES. Edited, with an Introduction, Notes, and full explanation of the metres, by JOHN W. WHITE, A. M., Professor of the Greek Language and Literature in Baldwin University. $1.20 $1.50

WILKIN'S MANUAL OF GREEK PROSE COMPOSITION. 1 vol. 12mo. Cloth 2.00 2.50

LATIN.

ALLEN & GREENOUGH'S LATIN GRAMMAR. Founded on Comparative Grammar. By J. H. ALLEN, Cambridge, and J. B. GREENOUGH, Instructor in Latin in Harvard College, and Lecturer on Comparative Philology in the University course. pp. 263 . . . . . . 1.25 1.56

"A complete Latin Grammar to be used from the beginning of the study of Latin till the end of the college course." The forms of the language and the constructions of Syntax are fully illustrated by classical examples and by comparison with parallel forms of kindred languages.

ALLEN & GREENOUGH'S SELECT ORATIONS OF CICERO. Chronologically arranged, covering the entire period of his Public Life. Edited by J. H. & W. F. ALLEN and J. B. GREENOUGH, with References to Allen & Greenough's Latin Grammar. Containing the Defence of Roscius (abridged), Verres I., Manilian Law, Catiline, Archias, Sestius (abridged), Milo, Marcellus, Ligarius, and the Fourteenth Philippic. With Life, Introductions, Notes, and Index 1.40 1.75

ALLEN & GREENOUGH'S VIRGIL. Containing the Bucolics and six books of the Æneid 1.40 1.75

ALLEN & GREENOUGH'S SALLUST'S CATILINE. 60 1.00

ALLEN & GREENOUGH'S CICERO DE SENECTUTE (Cato Major), in uniform style with Allen & Greenough's Cicero. 1 vol. 12mo. Cloth . . . . .60 .75

ALLEN & GREENOUGH'S SHORTER COURSE OF LATIN PROSE: Consisting chiefly of the Prose Selections of Allen's Latin Reader (to p. 134), the Notes being wholly rewritten, enlarged, and adapted to Allen & Greenough's Grammar; accompanied by Six Orations of Cicero, — the Manilian, the four Catilines, and Archias, — thus forming a volume adapted to the second or shorter preparatory course at Harvard, with Vocabulary. . 2.00 2.50

ALLEN & GREENOUGH'S LATIN SELECTIONS. With full Notes and References to Allen & Greenough's Grammar . . 1.25 1.56

ALLEN & GREENOUGH'S CÆSAR (Gallic War, Four Books). With very full Notes, Maps, and References to their Grammar as well as Gildersleeve's 1.25 1.56
    Do. without Vocabulary 1.00 1.25

ALLEN'S LATIN READER. 12mo 518 pages. Consisting of Selections from Cæsar, Curtius, Nepos, Sallust, Ovid, Virgil, Plautus, Terence, Cicero, Pliny, and Tacitus, with Notes, and a general Vocabulary of Latin of more than 16,000 words 2.00 2.50

ALLEN'S LATIN LEXICON. 12mo. 205 pages. (Being the Vocabulary to the Reader.) Cloth 1.00 1.25

ALLEN'S LATIN PRIMER. A First Book of Latin for Boys and Girls. By J. H ALLEN. 155 pages. Cloth . . . 1.00 1.25

This is designed for the use of scholars of a younger class, and consists of thirty lessons, carefully arranged (an adaptation of the Robertsonian method) so as to give a full outline of the Grammar accompanied by Tables of Inflection, with Dialogues

	Wholesale.	Retail.

ALLEN'S LATIN COMPOSITION. Adapted to Allen & Greenough's Latin Grammar. By W. F. ALLEN. 107 pages. Cloth . $1.00 $1.25

This book includes a careful review of the Principles of Syntax, as contained in the Grammar, with practice in various styles of composition (from classical models), Vocabulary, and Parallel References to other Grammars.

ALLEN'S MANUAL LATIN GRAMMAR. Prepared by W. F. and J. H. ALLEN. 12mo. 148 pages, with Index. Cloth . 1.00 1.25

Approved by Harvard College as indicating the amount required for admission.

ALLEN'S LATIN LESSONS. 12mo. 134 pages . . 1.00 1.25

LEIGHTON'S LATIN LESSONS. Prepared to accompany Allen & Greenough's Latin Grammar. By R. F. LEIGHTON, Melrose High School.

This work presents a progressive series of exercises (both Latin and English), illustrating the grammatical forms and simpler principles of syntax. Synonymes and rules of quantity are introduced from the first. The text consists of about a dozen of Æsop's Fables, translated from the Greek for these Lessons; extracts from L'Homond's Viri Romae (Romulus and Remus); Horatii and Curatii; Lives of Cato, Pompey, Cæsar, Cicero, Brutus, and Augustus; the Helvetian War, from Woodford's Epitome of Cæsar. All fully illustrated with Notes, References, and Maps. Full Vocabularies accompany the book, with questions for Examination and Review of the Grammar 1.25 1.56

MADVIG'S LATIN GRAMMAR. Carefully revised by THOMAS A. THACHER, Yale College. Half morocco 2.40 3.00

The most complete and valuable Treatise on the language yet published, and admirably adapted to the wants of Teachers and College Classes.

THE LATIN VERB. Illustrated by the Sanskrit. By C. H. PARKHURST. Cloth . . . . .40 .50

WHITE'S JUNIOR STUDENT'S COMPLETE LATIN-ENGLISH LEXICON. Morocco back 2.40 3.00
Sheep 2.50 3.50

WHITE'S JUNIOR STUDENT'S COMPLETE LATIN-ENGLISH AND ENGLISH-LATIN LEXICON. By the REV. J. T. WHITE, D. D., of C. C. C. Oxford, Rector of St. Martin, Ludgate, London. Revised Edition. Square 12mo. pp. 1058. Sheep 3.60 4.50

"The present work aims at furnishing in both its parts a sufficiently extensive vocabulary for all practical purposes. The Latin words and phrases are in all cases followed by the name of some standard Latin writer, as a guaranty of their authority; and as the work is of a strictly elementary character, the conjugations of the verbs and the genders and genitive cases of the substantives are uniformly added. In the preparation of this portion of the book, DR. WHITE has had the assistance of some of the best scholars both of Oxford and Cambridge." — *Guardian.*

WHITE'S JUNIOR STUDENT'S COMPLETE ENGLISH-LATIN LEXICON. Sheep 2.00 2.50

We have contracted with Messrs. Longmans, Green, & Co., of London, for the sole agency in this country for the above Latin Lexicons, and shall endeavor to meet the demands of the trade.

THE ŒDIPUS TYRANNUS OF SOPHOCLES. Edited, with an Introduction, Notes, and full explanation of the metres, by JOHN W. WHITE, A. M., Professor of the Greek Language and Literature in Baldwin University. $1.20 $1.50

WILKIN'S MANUAL OF GREEK PROSE COMPOSITION. 1 vol. 12mo. Cloth 2.00 2.50

LATIN.

ALLEN & GREENOUGH'S LATIN GRAMMAR. Founded on Comparative Grammar. By J. H. ALLEN, Cambridge, and J. B. GREENOUGH, Instructor in Latin in Harvard College, and Lecturer on Comparative Philology in the University course. pp. 263 . . . . . . 1.25 1.56

"A complete Latin Grammar to be used from the beginning of the study of Latin till the end of the college course." The forms of the language and the constructions of Syntax are fully illustrated by classical examples and by comparison with parallel forms of kindred languages.

ALLEN & GREENOUGH'S SELECT ORATIONS OF CICERO. Chronologically arranged, covering the entire period of his Public Life. Edited by J. H. & W. F. ALLEN and J. B. GREENOUGH, with References to Allen & Greenough's Latin Grammar. Containing the Defence of Roscius (abridged), Verres I., Manilian Law, Catiline, Archias, Sestius (abridged), Milo, Marcellus, Ligarius, and the Fourteenth Philippic. With Life, Introductions, Notes, and Index 1.40 1.75

ALLEN & GREENOUGH'S VIRGIL. Containing the Bucolics and six books of the Æneid 1.40 1.75

ALLEN & GREENOUGH'S SALLUST'S CATILINE. 80 1.00

ALLEN & GREENOUGH'S CICERO DE SENECTUTE (Cato Major), in uniform style with Allen & Greenough's Cicero. 1 vol. 12mo. Cloth .60 .75

ALLEN & GREENOUGH'S SHORTER COURSE OF LATIN PROSE: Consisting chiefly of the Prose Selections of Allen's Latin Reader (to p. 134), the Notes being wholly rewritten, enlarged, and adapted to Allen & Greenough's Grammar; accompanied by Six Orations of Cicero, — the Manilian, the four Catilines, and Archias, — thus forming a volume adapted to the second or shorter preparatory course at Harvard, with Vocabulary. . 2.00 2.50

ALLEN & GREENOUGH'S LATIN SELECTIONS. With full Notes and References to Allen & Greenough's Grammar . . 1.25 1.56

ALLEN & GREENOUGH'S CÆSAR (Gallic War, Four Books). With very full Notes, Maps, and References to their Grammar as well as Gildersleeve's 1.25 1.56
    Do. without Vocabulary 1.00 1.25

ALLEN'S LATIN READER. 12mo 518 pages. Consisting of Selections from Cæsar, Curtius, Nepos, Sallust, Ovid, Virgil, Plautius, Terence, Cicero, Pliny, and Tacitus, with Notes, and a general Vocabulary of Latin of more than 16,000 words 2.00 2.50

ALLEN'S LATIN LEXICON. 12mo. 205 pages. (Being the Vocabulary to the Reader.) Cloth 1.00 1.25

ALLEN'S LATIN PRIMER. A First Book of Latin for Boys and Girls. By J. H ALLEN. 155 pages. Cloth . . . 1.00 1.25

This is designed for the use of scholars of a younger class, and consists of thirty lessons, carefully arranged (an adaptation of the Robertsonian method) so as to give a full outline of the Grammar accompanied by Tables of Inflection, with Dialogues (Latin and English), and Selections for reading.

	Wholesale.	Retail.

ALLEN'S LATIN COMPOSITION. Adapted to Allen & Greenough's Latin Grammar. By W. F. ALLEN. 107 pages. Cloth . $1.00 $1.25

This book includes a careful review of the Principles of Syntax, as contained in the Grammar, with practice in various styles of composition (from classical models), Vocabulary, and Parallel References to other Grammars.

ALLEN'S MANUAL LATIN GRAMMAR. Prepared by W. F. and J. H. ALLEN. 12mo. 148 pages, with Index. Cloth . . 1.00 1.25

Approved by Harvard College as indicating the amount required for admission.

ALLEN'S LATIN LESSONS. 12mo. 134 pages . . 1.00 1.25

LEIGHTON'S LATIN LESSONS. Prepared to accompany Allen & Greenough's Latin Grammar. By R. F. LEIGHTON, Melrose High School.

This work presents a progressive series of exercises (both Latin and English), illustrating the grammatical forms and simpler principles of syntax. Synonymes and rules of quantity are introduced from the first. The text consists of about a dozen of Æsop's Fables, translated from the Greek for these Lessons; extracts from L'Homond's Viri Romæ (Romulus and Remus); Horatii and Curatii; Lives of Cato, Pompey, Cæsar, Cicero, Brutus, and Augustus; the Helvetian War, from Woodford's Epitome of Cæsar. All fully illustrated with Notes, References, and Maps. Full Vocabularies accompany the book, with questions for Examination and Review of the Grammar 1.25 1.56

MADVIG'S LATIN GRAMMAR. Carefully revised by THOMAS A. THACHER, Yale College. Half morocco . . . 2.40 3.00

The most complete and valuable Treatise on the language yet published, and admirably adapted to the wants of Teachers and College Classes.

THE LATIN VERB. Illustrated by the Sanskrit. By C. H. PARKHURST. Cloth . . . . .40 .50

WHITE'S JUNIOR STUDENT'S COMPLETE LATIN-ENGLISH LEXICON. Morocco back 2.40 3.00
Sheep 2.80 3.50

WHITE'S JUNIOR STUDENT'S COMPLETE LATIN-ENGLISH AND ENGLISH-LATIN LEXICON. By the REV. J. T. WHITE, D. D., of C. C. C. Oxford, Rector of St. Martin, Ludgate, London. Revised Edition. Square 12mo. pp. 1058. Sheep . . . 3.60 4.50

"The present work aims at furnishing in both its parts a sufficiently extensive vocabulary for all practical purposes. The Latin words and phrases are in all cases followed by the name of some standard Latin writer, as a guaranty of their authority; and as the work is of a strictly elementary character, the conjugations of the verbs and the genders and genitive cases of the substantives are uniformly added. In the preparation of this portion of the book, DR. WHITE has had the assistance of some of the best scholars both of Oxford and Cambridge." — *Guardian.*

WHITE'S JUNIOR STUDENT'S COMPLETE ENGLISH-LATIN LEXICON. Sheep 2.00 2.50

We have contracted with Messrs. Longmans, Green, & Co., of London, for the sole agency in this country for the above Latin Lexicons, and shall endeavor to meet the demands of the trade.

Wholesale. Retail

HUDSON'S SCHOOL SHAKESPEARE. 3d Series . . 2.00
Containing MIDSUMMER NIGHT'S DREAM, CYMBELINE,
MUCH ADO ABOUT NOTHING, CORIOLANUS,
KING HENRY VIII., OTHELLO, THE MOOR OF VENICE.
ROMEO AND JULIET,

SEPARATE PLAYS FROM HUDSON'S SCHOOL
SHAKESPEARE. In pamphlet form, 40 cents each.

AS YOU LIKE IT, MUCH ADO ABOUT NOTHING,
HENRY IV. Part I. ROMEO AND JULIET,
KING LEAR, OTHELLO,
THE MERCHANT OF VENICE, THE TEMPEST,
JULIUS CÆSAR, MACBETH,
HAMLET, HENRY VIII.

STEWART'S ELEMENTARY PHYSICS, with QUESTIONS AND EXERCISES. By PROF. G. A. HILL, of Harvard University.

The Questions will be direct and exhaustive upon the text of Mr. Stewart's work. After the Questions will be given a series of easy Exercises and Problems, designed, in the hands of a good teacher, to arouse and strengthen in the student's mind the power of reasoning in accordance with sound scientific methods.

THE ŒDIPUS TYRANNUS OF SOPHOCLES. Edited,
with an Introduction, Notes, and full explanation of the metres, by JOHN W. WHITE, A. M., Professor of the Greek language and literature in Baldwin University.

The text will depart as little as possible from MS authority. The Notes, with grammatical references to Goodwin and Hadley, will aim at giving the student all the help necessary to a clear understanding of the text.

The metres will be explained on the recently advanced theory of DR J HEINRICH SCHMIDT, of Berlin. To this end a considerably abridged translation of his "Leitfaden in der Rhythmik und Metrik" will be added to the Notes.

OUTLINES OF THE COMPARATIVE GRAMMAR OF
SANSKRIT, GREEK, AND LATIN, embracing in small compass the general principles of Etymology, with full references to authorities and larger works; designed as a text-book or for self-instruction. By J. B. GREENOUGH.

OUTLINES OF ASTRONOMY. By ARTHUR SEARLE, Assistant at Harvard College Observatory.

This work is intended to give such elementary instruction in the principal branches of Astronomy as is required in High Schools or by any students not far advanced in mathematics. It will be illustrated by engravings carefully prepared with a view to accuracy, and will contain some information on each of the following subjects: —

1. The chief results of astronomical inquiry up to the present time with regard to the general constitution of the universe, and, in particular, with regard to the stars, planets, nebulæ, comets, and meteors.
2. The methods of astronomical research, and their application to the arts.
3. The general principles of theoretical astronomy.
4. The history of astronomy.
5. Astronomical statistics.

AN INTRODUCTION TO THE STUDY OF THE
RHYTHM AND METRE OF THE CLASSICAL LANGUAGES, on the Theory of Dr. J. H. Heinrich Schmidt, of Berlin. To which will be added the Text of the Lyrical Parts of some of the more generally read of the Greek Dramas, with Rhythmical Schemes, and a Commentary. Edited by JOHN W. WHITE, A. M , Professor of the Greek Language and Literature in Baldwin University.

This work has been undertaken at the solicitation of certain eminent educators who have advised the editor to expand the Appendix on Rhythm and Metre which had been prepared for his forthcoming edition of the ŒDIPUS TYRANNUS OF SOPHOCLES into the volume now announced. The aim will be to present a clear and succinct dogmatic statement of the theory of Dr. Schmidt for the use of classes in the Greek and Latin poets. To be ready some time within the college year 1874-75.

RECENTLY ISSUED.

Wholesale. Retail

ALLEN & GREENOUGH'S SELECT ORATIONS OF CICERO. Chronologically Arranged; covering the entire period of his Public Life. Edited by J. H. & W. F. ALLEN, and J. B. GREENOUGH, with References to Allen & Greenough's Latin Grammar. Containing the Defence of Roscius (abridged), Verres I., Manilian Law, Catiline, Archias, Sestius (abridged), Milo, Marcellus, Ligarius, and the Fourteenth Philippic. With Life, Introductions, Notes, and Index $1.40 $1.75

This selection differs from other school editions of Cicero, in aiming to give a complete view of his career as an orator and a statesman. The Introduction contains a brief outline of his life, accompanied by a chronological table of events, and a full list of his extant orations, with their topics, occasions etc. The historical introductions to the special orations accompany the text, while the argument is given, so far as possible, in head-lines on the page, so as to afford the learner every help to the eye for easy comprehension. The text follows the most approved revision, that of Baiter and Kayser. The Notes are designed to give all the aid which will be of service to teacher or pupil, for an understanding of the language, style, and structure of the orations, and — besides full historical exposition of the text — are accompanied by numerous illustrations (in smaller type) of special points of history or antiquities; a full Index being given at the end. It is intended that, so far as possible within its limits, this volume shall supply all that the general student would seek in a complete and critical edition of the Orations.

ALLEN & GREENOUGH'S SHORTER COURSE OF LATIN PROSE: Consisting of Selections from Cæsar, Curtius, Nepos, and Sallust (Jugurtha), with Notes adapted to Allen & Greenough's Grammar; accompanied by Six Orations of Cicero, — the Manilian, the four Catilines, and Archias, — thus forming a volume adapted to the second or shorter preparatory course at Harvard. With Vocabulary $2.00 $2.50

ALLEN & GREENOUGH'S SELECTIONS. Consisting of Selections from Cæsar, Curtius, Nepos, and Sallust (Jugurtha), without Vocabulary.

HALSEY'S BIBLE CHART OF GENEALOGY AND CHRONOLOGY, from the Creation to A.D. 100. Prepared by C. S. HALSEY 1.00 1.25

This Chart is designed to illustrate Bible History by showing on a clear and simple plan the genealogy and chronology of the principal persons mentioned in the Scriptures.

HALSEY'S GENEALOGICAL AND CHRONOLOGICAL CHART, of the Rulers of England, Scotland, France, Germany, and Spain. By C. S. HALSEY. Mounted, 33 × 48 inches. Folded and Bound in 4to, 10 × 12 inches 1.50

VIENNA, AUSTRIA, August 4, 1873.

LUTHER WHITING MASON, ESQ.

DEAR SIR, — I am happy to inform you that the International Jury for Group 26, of the World's Exhibition, has seen fit to award you for your Method of Teaching Music, as illustrated in your Charts and Books, the high distinction of the MEDAL OF MERIT. In my judgment this is clearly a case in which honor has been rendered where honor was due. That you may long live to enjoy it, is the sincere wish of your friend, JOHN D. PHILBRICK.

GINN BROTHERS,
4 Beacon Street, Boston.

www.ingramcontent.com/pod-product-compliance
Lightning Source LLC
Chambersburg PA
CBHW030359170426
43202CB00010B/1424